One Night in the Desert, God Said…

An Unfolding Love Story about Restoration, Romance, and Rhema

Paul and Samantha Roach

To a wonderful ??? Person!! You are loved Dora.

Samantha

One Night in the Desert, God Said...

Readers may order copies by contacting the authors at faithfamilychurch@coxinet.net
P.O.B. 878, El Reno, Oklahoma 73036
1-800-611-4909 / 405-262-5509

Published and Printed By Dare 2 Dream Books
Mustang, Oklahoma
405-642-8257

Publisher's Cataloging in Publication
1. Counseling 2. Christian Counseling 3. Christianity 4. Marriage Counseling
ISBN 978-0-9779692-5-8

Forward by Kirk A. DuBois

Most of us can count on one hand the true friends in our lives that "stick closer than a brother." Paul is one of those in my life. From our early days as singles when we were roommates – hungry for the things of God, going to conferences, reading aloud to each other and wearing out copies of Smith Wigglesworth's books, giving them away and buying new ones, stepping out in faith together to follow God and seeing His supernatural provision again and again – to sharing our victories and battles with each other. We have a friendship like Jonathan and David. We can share our deepest hurts, secrets, hopes and dreams freely without any fear or distrust. (I often joke that we know too much on each other so we keep each other in line.)

As time passed by we drifted apart for a season while our paths sporadically crossed. I got married and eventually ended up back in Oklahoma and back in Paul's life. Our lives continued to intertwine again at RHEMA. There he met Samantha. We all developed new friendships there. The circled widened and soon Paul and Samantha were married. Now our lives are still intersecting – this time with our wives along side. Still, Paul & I maintain a close relationship in the Lord.

It has been a joy to see how God has given "beauty for ashes" in both Paul and Samantha's lives. I believe this book will encourage you in your own journey with the Lord. It will show you that God will never give up on you. Just don't give up on Him – or yourself!

For the gifts and calling of God *are* without repentance.
 Rom 11:29

Dedication

We've thought of all the people who've had a major impact on our lives and the question arose, "Whom do we dedicate this book to?"

There were so many, for both of us that helped us to get where we are now, but the one person that we keep coming back to is the Lord Jesus Christ. So to Jesus, who loved us even at our worst and forgave us, picked us up, cleaned us up and restored us, we dedicate this book.

Our prayer is that if you're reading this book and you're life has been like ours, know that Jesus Christ has not and will not give up on you. He still has a wonderful plan for your life. He's just waiting for you to come to Him and let him restore you and give you hope and a future In HIM.

Table of Contents

Acknowledgements

We want to say a heartfelt thank to all who helped in any way to bring this book to completion—especially, our Faith Family Church family.

There are also people mentioned in the book that had a major impact in our lives that we want to make sure are acknowledged:

Rhema Bible Training Center and Pastor Ken and Lynette Hagin, Broken Arrow, OK, www.rhema.org 918-258-1588

Pastor David Ingles / Walnut Grove Church, Broken Arrow, OK, www.oasisnetwork.org

Song: "I Sure Love You" from the album, "I Sure Love You" by David Ingles

Song: "Life Is Big, Rich, and Wonderful," from the album, "El Shaddai" by David Ingles

The Day of New Beginnings

The following has been adapted from a classic poem by Louise Fletcher:

I wish that there were some wonderful place
Called the Land of Beginning Again
Where all our mistakes
And all our heartaches
And the worst of that we had done
Could be dropped
Like a shabby old coat by the door
And never be put on again.
For what had been hardest,
We'd know had been best,
And what had seemed loss would be gain.
And we would start over hand in hand
In the Land of Beginning Again.

This adapted poem is quoted here because it is the proper beginning for the story that is about to unfold in the following pages. Two lives, lived separately for years physically, yet joined together by God spiritually, travel a journey separate yet together, different yet the same. Two lives that struggled with

7

their relationship with God struggled alone yet with a common bond. Both were on a journey that drew them closer to God and in doing so drew them closer to each other. The journey was from a land of failure and poor choices for both, but the journey was to a land of new beginnings, where God makes all things new.

Many have traveled the road from California to Oklahoma and from Oklahoma to California, but only these two lives traveled this unique journey of ordained destiny.

The journey or journeys would culminate at Rhema Bible Training Center, not only for the purpose of marriage, but also for a greater and more glorious journey in the Kingdom of God. The road to Rhema was bumpy to say the least, and so has been the road from Rhema. The difference is not in the bumps; the difference is in whom you share those bumps with.

One Night in the Desert, God Said... will not only touch your heart, it will renew your belief in God and challenge your commitment to seeking and being in the Will of God. Join us on this incredible journey.

Dearly Beloved We Are Gathered Here

The moment of truth had finally arrived. In just a few minutes I, Paul Roach, would take Samantha as my wife. This was it! This was the day God had planned for me to marry the girl of my dreams. Don't misunderstand; it wasn't the moment of truth for me, it was the moment of truth for my bride. I stood at the front of the church anxiously awaiting the appearance of my soon-to-be wife, all dressed in white, to walk down the aisle and join me.

All the groomsmen, dressed in their handsome tuxedos with some completing their fashionable ensemble with white socks to complement their black tuxedos, had taken their place along side of me. The beautiful bridesmaids and the maid of honor had all flawlessly walked down the aisle clothed with beautiful gowns arraying their beauty. Little did we know that some of the dresses were held together by safety pins because the seamstress didn't finish the dresses in time for the wedding. Just moments before, she was frantically finishing the dresses while they were on the attendants using pins instead of thread.

There we were, all seventeen of us—myself, eight bridesmaids and eight groomsmen—waiting for the bride to make her magnificent entrance into the church sanctuary.

There had been a few minor crises that day that we had survived. For instance, the man who was to videotape the wedding was found stranded on the highway by Samantha and Leslie, one of the bridesmaids, on their way to the church. They threw his equipment into their car and together rushed to the church—it was a good thing that this was the wedding God had planned. The fact that the man was dressed in a beautiful Hawaiian shirt that stood out like a neon sign went well with the white socks worn by some of my groomsmen.

One of the singers, a girl who had been in my youth group in San Diego and was attending Oral Roberts University, had a horrible sore throat. She could hardly talk, and she wanted to bless us and sing anyway.

Back to the moment of truth. I was confident and unwavering that Samantha was to be my wife. Ever since one night in the desert when God and I had an encounter, there was no doubt that she was chosen by God to complete me. With Samantha, her confidence waned from time to time—our wedding day just happened to be one of those days. But I think Samantha should tell it in her own words.

(Samantha) The photographer, Glenn, was taking all the pre-wedding pictures and had just finished photographing the guys. I walked out from my dressing room and saw Paul's uncle, Ted, who looked so much like Paul that I thought it was Paul. I backed up and thought, "Oh, no! He's not supposed to see me before the wedding!" Then all of the sudden, I had a moment of sheer panic! I thought, "Oh, God! Oh, God! What am I doing? Oh God, I can't do this! How in the world can I do this? Am I sure this is right? I can't afford to miss it again." I'd been married two times before, both out of the will of God and had made such a mess out of my life before, and I did not want to mess up again. In fact, I had been so scared that I almost called the wedding off three times because of my fear of missing God's will. "Did I hear God right?" I told myself that I just didn't know.

But I did know. I had heard God. He had given supernatural signs all the way through our engagement. The problem was I had been burning the candle at both ends for almost a year. I had been doing singles activities at Walnut Grove for David Ingles, plus I'd gone to work for Rhema full time, and was teaching self-image classes on the side. I had gotten into what I call a "busier than God" mode. I wasn't spending the time in prayer that I needed to. That's so important you know. People get in trouble when they make decisions based on feelings and not on

11

listening to their spirit. So here I am, out in the hallway, panic written all over my face, thinking, "I am changing my life forever! Am I doing the right thing?"

Glen and his wife saw me. They grabbed me and shook me, "This is not the time to panic! You are getting married today. You are going to marry the man of your dreams. You do not want to mess up your wedding pictures! Now get yourself together!"

I wanted to be a beautiful, gracious bride, but instead, I was trying to get fear out of me. I think Glen and his wife brought me back to reality. I finally made it to the sanctuary entrance. From this point I think Paul's observation captures the moment well from his vantage point as he waited for his bride.

(Paul) I was standing with the wedding party waiting for that glorious moment of seeing my beautiful bride for the first time on our wedding day. Finally she comes in with her dad. It had been pretty comical so far. We had one of those carpets that the guys unrolled down the middle isle for the bride to walk down and it wouldn't roll out right. Then she started coming down the aisle and I noticed that she was scared spitless. She was looking everywhere but at me. My thought was, "She looks like a guppy!" Her mouth was going like she was gasping for air—she was hyper-ventilating or something.

My heart went out to her and I tried to make eye contact to assure her that everything was okay. Instead, her next move left me a bit nervous. Nobody had informed me that Glen had told her and her dad to stop halfway down the aisle and look over their shoulders so he could take their picture together. She forgot and her dad whispered to her, so finally they stopped and looked back and I was thinking, "What is she doing? Oh my God, is she gonna bolt?" I'm seriously thinking, "If she starts to run, I'm going to run her down!" I thought to myself, "I have a runaway bride on my hands!"

She wouldn't look at me. I knew if she would just look at me she'd be okay. When they got to the front, she was still looking like a guppy but finally she looked at me, and you could just see this peace come over her. As she looked at me she started smiling, and I was smiling back at her, and then she was fine.

I knew Samantha had some tough bouts of questioning and fear, but I never wavered in my belief that this woman and only this woman was chosen by God as my wife. I knew that in the past, every week that I'd go up to Rhema to be with her, God would literally give me the things I needed to tell her to bring her peace. When I would leave she would wrestle again with a new fear. I also knew in my heart that Satan would do whatever possible to sabotage our wedding, but I also knew that it wasn't going to happen.

On our wedding day the last battle was fought as Samantha made her way to marry the man God had chosen for her. Once our hands were joined together, no man and no power could separate us. I knew the moment we joined hands that today was worth the journey, and the promise of what was ahead far overshadowed what was behind us.

The Journey Begins

Samantha's Story 1971-1976

For I know the plans I have for you, declares the Lord, plans to prosper you and not to harm you, plans to give you hope and a future. Jeremiah 29:11 (NIV)

I was living in Santa Ana, California, and in April of 1971 I had just come back to the Lord while in Escondido, California. Just forty miles away Paul had started his work as a youth minister in San Diego. We didn't know each other and wouldn't meet until 1982. But God knew both of us, and His plan would unfold as both of us began our journey to Rhema Bible Training Center in Broken Arrow, Oklahoma.

1971 was a turning point in my life. God had become very important to me. My husband had left me for his secretary and had moved back to San Francisco, and I didn't know what to do with that. It would have been nice to be free of him and his abusive ways, but it seemed like everybody that I was around at the time told me I shouldn't think thoughts like freedom and new beginnings, but rather, according to

15

the group I was a part of at that time, I was to believe God for my husband to come back.

He did return, and I took him back because that was the "Christian" thing to do. Perhaps that was what God desired and what some said the Bible taught, but for me it was a prison I was destined to waste away in. Throughout our rocky marriage, he would ask me to leave over and over again. When he got tired of me being gone, he would move heaven and earth to get me to come back. Twice he went to my pastor and twice I was told that I would have to stay with him if that was what he wanted. My pastor would use the scripture in 1 Corinthians 7:13 where Paul wrote, "And a woman hath a husband that believes not, and if he be pleased to dwell with her, let her not leave him" (KJV).

So the pattern continued. We would be separated a few months, and then he would want me to come back. The pastor would tell me that he had prayed the sinner's prayer and everything would be all right. But, it was hard going back. I would be scared at night to be with him, but according to my church, I was obligated to go back.

I wanted to do God's will. I was serving God with everything that was in me. One night—a church night—he tore up my Bible to keep me from going to church, but I had determined in my heart that I was going to church no matter what he did. We would get into knockdown, drag-out fights on Sundays and Wednesdays, but we never fought on any other day or night—only Sunday mornings, Sunday nights, and Wednesday nights. The truth is that he was never there any other time of the week, but he was always there on church days or nights to fight me about going.

A conference I had gone to gave me the impression that I was to obey my husband no matter what. If he wanted to drag me to pornographic movies or go to gay bars and all kinds of God-dishonoring things, I was told that I was to be submissive. I wanted to obey God and I wanted to serve my Lord. If only I had known then what God has taught me over the years.

In January of 1972, shortly after moving to San Francisco, I was walking downtown near Fillmore West where there was a big rock star event going on. There was a big crowd, and of course police were everywhere. While I was studying the crowd, with a policeman standing no more than two feet away from me, somebody approached me about buying drugs. Here were all these young people caught up in a world of drugs and hard rock. I got to thinking about the need for Christian entertainment and the need for churches to provide fun, upbeat activities for young Christians to enjoy. I remember wondering at the time what my future as a Christian held.

That night at about 2 a.m., I woke up and sat straight up in bed. I saw myself on a stage with someone, and I had the impression that the person was my husband. In the vision I was in a big place, kind of a half-circle type room, and people were coming down to the front in droves—people from all backgrounds. We were praying with them and they were getting saved.

While this man and I were praying with the people, someone rolled out a portable baptismal tank. The people were getting dressed in white robes, and the man I was with got into the baptismal tank and baptized all these people who came up out of the water speaking in tongues.

I somehow knew that the man in the vision was my husband. Later I asked people in church about the vision, and they told me that it could only mean that my husband was going to get saved. People would tell me, "God wouldn't show you that you are to marry another man. You need to stay with your husband." Talk about a mixed reaction to such an awesome vision. God was showing me that I would be serving Him in a mighty way and according to them it would be with the man that was abusing me.

I kept the vision in my heart. Years later I came to understand that the man I was serving with in the vision was the man that God *was* preparing to be my husband and that we would share in a wonderful ministry, side-by-side.

Allow me to fast forward to September of 1976. I was standing in my kitchen overlooking the back yard. I heard the Lord say to me, "Could you leave all this?" The "all this" God was talking about was about $950,000.00 in real estate holdings, including our home just freshly decorated to my taste, the custom designed swimming pool with an Olympic size swimming lane and a six seat Jacuzzi in my back yard. I had just purchased beautiful sterling silverware and had just paid off my car.

Could I leave all of that? I knew it was the Lord speaking, and I took the question seriously. I began to ponder my life with Ray. I thought about the abuse I had endured through the years. A lot of women could tell you about their black eyes and bloody faces. Although I had some physical abuse, I dealt mostly with emotional and verbal abuse. I had gotten to a place where I was afraid to even speak for fear it wasn't correct enough English for him. I had learned not to do anything that would cause him to be violent to me. There were times he would tell me that my price on the streets of San Francisco was a hundred dollars. He would say, "I can pay someone a hundred dollars, and he could walk up to you in a crowd and shoot you and then melt into the crowd and never be

19

found." I would walk around every day wondering if that was the day I was going to be shot.

In order to handle the difficulties of my life, I had developed a habit of thinking of other people who suffered far worse abuse than me. At that time the Iron Curtain of Russia hadn't yet fallen. I would remind myself that my situation was nowhere near as bad as the persecution those people suffered under. I convinced myself that if they could suffer under such great persecution, I could suffer through the abuse at home and somehow that gave me strength to handle what I was dealing with.

So when God asked me that question, I don't know why I knew, but I just knew that it was a serious question. If God were to provide a way of escape, would I be willing to go and leave behind nearly one-million dollars of investments that I had helped build? I thought, "Yes, I could," and would leave it all, because I would be among Christians. The pastors I had at that time had closed our church and moved to Seattle, Washington, and I knew in my heart that if I ever left Ray, I would be moving there. Yes, I was willing. My heart belonged to Him, my Lord and Savior, and I trusted that what would be ahead with God as my guide would be far better than all the riches in the world.

Reflections from Samantha

What do I want you to learn from this chapter of my life? I love to look back and relive those wonderful miraculous things that God did to put our marriage together; but the most important part of this book is to help you not make the mistakes that we made.

If you've already made those mistakes, then the important thing to know is that there is hope for you. You need to know that God is in the forgiving business, and a God of new beginnings. I had been married twice. Both times were out of the will of God. I was backslidden in sin, committing adultery and an alcoholic involved in many other things that that were wrong.

You need to know that not only does God forgive; He is in the "restoration" business. The day I turned my life back over to the Lord, I had been in bed with my boss. My husband was somewhere sleeping with someone else. I remember waking up, getting dressed, and looking at the guy I was with and thinking, "I can't do this anymore. This is not right. I know better." I told God that I was burning my bridges behind me, and I was never going to look back. I asked Him to put within me whatever it took to serve Him all the rest of my life. That was many years ago. He has been absolutely faithful, to keep me on track and to put me where I needed to be to receive the teaching I needed to walk in victory. Corrie Ten Boome sums up my experience with these words, 'There is no pit so deep that God's love is not deeper still." Truly, His grace is both sufficient and abundant.

The first lesson the Lord taught me was during one night during that first week back with the Lord. My husband left me for his secretary. They left me without a car, without food in the house, and without any money—those were days before we started making money. If I didn't have a car, I was going to lose my job. I remember crying all evening. I felt like I cried a river of tears. I paced the living room up and down. I would glance at my Bible and the Lord would say, "Open your Bible."

I remember thinking several times, "There's no way that there is anything in there that will help me with what I'm feeling. Still, the voice was persistent. Finally, exhausted, I grabbed my Bible and angrily cried out, "Alright, Lord! There better be something on the first page I open!" I sat down, opened my Bible, and began reading, "Now faith is the substance of things hoped for, the evidence of things not seen." It was the 11th chapter of Hebrews, known to most as the "Faith" chapter.

When I finished reading that chapter, I knew God loved me. I knew He knew my name and that He knew what I was going through. I knew that whatever befell me in life, God was bigger than any problem that would come my way. By the end of the week, God had not only supplied me with a car and food, but also with money to tide me over.

The most important lesson I learned that week was that the Word of God is more vital than life itself. God taught me that whatever my need, if I would put Him and His Word first, He would supply answers, peace, strength, direction, and whatever it was that I needed in order to overcome.

Putting God first means everything else comes second. A couple of weeks later Ray came back, and I was told I had to accept him back. He would keep me out all night Saturday nights going to bars and parties. Sunday morning, I would be tired and it was so tempting to stay in bed and make excuses not to go to church. The one thing I knew was that I did not want to backslide again. Missing one Sunday would lead to another Sunday, then another, until one day I would look back and not be in church again. I could not take that road again.

The Lord impressed on me how vital it was that I be in church and in fellowship with other believers. Hebrews 10:25 states, "Not forsaking the assembling of ourselves together, as the manner of some is, but exhorting one another and so much more as ye see the day approaching." There were many days I would go to church, exhausted, discouraged, and feeling like I didn't have the strength to get through one more day. Invariably, the pastor always had a message that spoke directly to me. I often felt like he had been living in my back pocket. Not only that, but there would be people God would direct to speak to me and give me a word of encouragement that would be what I needed to get me through some very difficult times. Had I not gone to church I would not have received what I needed to help me overcome during that week.

We're not only to receive from others, but also to be a blessing to them. We often think we don't have anything to give to others because we feel so needy ourselves. The truth is that many times, just a smile or a personal, "I'm so glad to see you" ministers encouragement in ways that you don't ever know.

One time I came to church really discouraged because of all the fighting just to get to church that morning. I was fighting tears back, and someone came up to me and told me that my faithfulness to be in church was an encouragement to her to be faithful. I didn't know that, but it brightened my day. My faithfulness had ministered to someone. You have things in you that need to be shared with others. We all need to be encouraging one another, no matter how young in the Lord we might be.

The Journey Begins

Paul's Story 1971-1976

For I know the plans I have for you, declares the Lord, plans to prosper you and not to harm you, plans to give you hope and a future. Jeremiah 29:11 (NIV)

Hidden in the Arbuckle Mountains of Southern Oklahoma, Falls Creek is a Baptist encampment where thousands of young people go every summer and where multitudes of youth are called into the ministry. In the summer of 1967, I was one of those that God called. After a week long experience with God, I left camp excited that I was right in the center of God's will for my life. I came home from camp right in the middle of a church split.

While my youth group was at Falls Creek finding God, the deacons of my home church were ignoring God and plotting to fire my pastor. Here I was excited about preaching and becoming a minister, and I come home right in the middle of a mess. I kind of floundered for several months. Then we got a new pastor that took me under his wing and really helped me get solid again. That was the summer of '67. The fall of '68 found me at Central State, a small college in Edmond, Oklahoma.

My parents were poor, and I was the oldest of five, so college for me was all about scholarships; I had to have a scholarship. I had several offers to attend different colleges on a football scholarship including Oklahoma State, The University of Oklahoma, and the University of Arkansas. But after a lot of prayer with my father, I had peace about going to Central State in Edmond, Oklahoma, where I was able to start as defensive nose guard as a freshman. I must confess that it wasn't easy living up to my call to the ministry at a state college. In fact, I spent almost every night at the chapel during the first year there just praying. God honored my faithfulness, and in my second year at Central, a revival broke out within the team. It started with two guys I had led to the Lord, and from those two guys the revival spread like a wild fire. During that awesome time of revival, there were about 16 teammates who had received the Lord.

The same thing was happening at the Edmond High School's *Young Life Club*. I was also working there at that time. We were having a move of God, and a lot of kids got saved. Many of those kids are still serving God today, and many have stayed in contact with me over the years.

The summer of 1970, I had a chance to go to Boston and work in a Christian coffee house or go to

Duncan, Oklahoma and be youth pastor for the summer. I chose Duncan, and while there, was ordained to the ministry. In order to form a bond with some of the football players in Duncan, I worked out with them lifting weights, hoping to stay in shape myself. We got into a touch football game, and I blew my knee out—I mean I just blew it out big time. When I reported back to college my coaches were pretty upset with me about the knee. They encouraged me to go ahead and play through the season, and then, at the end of the season get an operation. I had seen several guys do that and they were in agony, and I was convinced it was not the right thing to do.

During that time God began dealing with me about immediately going into fulltime ministry and pulling out as a college junior. I had very strong Christian coaches, and one coach, Val Renol, prayed with me concerning my struggle and I chose to quit college and enter the ministry fulltime. It was one of the hardest things I ever did in my life because I was not a quitter. I had never quit anything. But I knew I had to obey God; I had to do what God wanted me to do.

While serving in Duncan, a young evangelist, Richard Hogue, a very good friend of mine, was using me a lot to give my testimony as an athlete in his *Sporinos*—Spiritual Revolution Now—meetings all over the country. Richard was holding a meeting at First Baptist Church of Rush Springs, just north of

Duncan, so I took my entire youth group up and during the meeting, gave my testimony.

Richard introduced me to the pastor, Buster Reeves, and we became very good friends. Not long after that, Buster became pastor of the First Baptist Church, Allied Gardens in San Diego, and contacted me about becoming his youth pastor. I wasn't sure about going to California—I was a farm boy from Oklahoma. But the church flew me out for a youth revival. That evening I met most of the kids who were part of the small youth group. While there that week, God just touched my heart tremendously, and I knew that I was supposed to go to California and become the youth pastor. It was January of 1971. I came back home, loaded up my car, and headed to California.

While there God did some wonderful things. Within a year and a half, we witnessed about 500 professions of faith and roughly half of them were teenagers and kids. During that short period of time, we were the fastest growing Southern Baptist Church in southern California.

We were doing everything that I had learned about being a successful church, but I was unhappy, worn out, and fed up. I was fed up with kids and fed up with parents. We had a youth church on Saturday night and would pack it out— sometimes seeing over 200 in attendance. We would have kids being saved all the time. But it wasn't enough. Chasing kids every week and keeping the kids away from drugs was a full time job in itself.

One night was particularly frustrating. It was one of *those* times with one of *those* parents. I had gone to visit one of my young people. He was very spoiled, but very sincere. He was a brand new Christian and very excited about learning about God and excited that I had come to visit him.

He invited me in and took me to meet his parents who were quite wealthy. They were sitting in the living room with other friends who were all sipping martinis. The boy introduced me as his youth pastor and the mother, who was sitting on the couch, said very sarcastically, "I don't want my child on Jesus. I would rather have him smoking marijuana and doing drugs than doing that Jesus thing." You could see that she was intoxicated, and in addition, she was belligerent. The husband apologized, but I left even more frustrated and discouraged.

One night later that week I went back to the church. San Diego is all mountains and canyons and the church was on the side of a hill overlooking the Charger Padre Stadium. You could literally look down into the stadium. I stood there in the dark crying as I looked down on the tops of the houses and the stadium; I was bawling my eyes out. At that point I had had it, and I felt I had no more to give.

I prayed to God and said, "I can't take this anymore, and it is only going to get worse. If this is the way that it is, God, if this is all there is to the ministry, I want out. I can't carry this. It's killing me. These kids are killing me. They're breaking my heart." As I stood there praying; I cried out, "Lord, if there is more to the ministry, if there is more to You, then show me."

This is where my dear friend, Kirk DuBois, came into my life. It was about two weeks later. He was a long-haired hippy about eighteen years old. Kirk was dating a girl in my youth group. He had been running with a rough group and doing things like breaking into his old junior high school and setting it on fire.

He and some friends had driven up the coast to a Taco Bell and had purchased drugs. While they were there sitting on a curb, a little Mexican man came up to them and started sharing the story of Jesus and passing out tracts. And so this man talked to him about Jesus and salvation, and told Kirk to read the tract. He asked if he wanted to accept Christ. Kirk didn't want to say "yes" because he feared what his friends would think. But he didn't want to say "no" because he knew in his heart that's what he wanted.

In California one of the big things was to go out to the beach all night and build a big fire and get high and drunk and all that stuff. Kirk said he took some drugs but nothing happened. His friends were wasted but he was still okay. He sat there reading the a New Testament he had taken with him and never did get high.

The next day while browsing through a Christian publication Kirk had received previously, he found the name of a place called *The Fish House* on El Cajon Boulevard and their telephone number. He called and got hold of a man by the name of Jim Roche—who became a very good friend of mine and a few years later helped to restore me when I was going through some troubled times. So Kirk went to the Fish House to meet with Jim. Jim starts going through the plan of salvation, and Kirk says, "You don't have to convince me, tell me what I need to do." They knelt down and prayed, and Kirk was saved right there. His life dramatically changed. A couple weeks later he was baptized in the ocean. Later that night they prayed for him and some others to receive the Holy Spirit. He received it by faith and about two weeks later he received his prayer language at home sitting on his bed.

Kirk was dating Laurie, and he started coming to the youth group. He had become what we called a "Jesus Freak" back in those days. He was on fire for God. He carried his Bible everywhere. He talked about Jesus to everybody. He had been baptized in the ocean and he spoke in tongues—and that was of the devil you know—so I didn't want him around the kids. The only problem was that being around Laurie, he was around the kids a lot.

In hindsight, what I thought was a problem was rather the Hand of God. Kirk's impact on the lives of my youth group, many of them troubled and constantly in trouble, was life-transforming. These kids got filled with the Holy Ghost and I argued with Kirk all of the time about doctrine, but something happened to these kids that I just couldn't argue with.

I was still frustrated with the ministry and Kirk. But, now the aggravation had changed, and Kirk literally was the answer to my desperate prayers even though I didn't see it at the time. Suddenly, I was seeing these kids change before my eyes—and a lot of parents were disturbed. You know when you get a whole section of your Baptist youth group speaking in tongues, glorifying God, and witnessing, you can be sure good Baptist parents will get really upset about it.

My problems were compounded because the parents didn't get mad at Kirk; they got mad at me, *and I didn't have anything to do with it.* These kids became very radical. Before, I would have to hand-lead them to do anything, and suddenly there was a radical transformation. They were praying as well as reading and carrying their Bibles around. They were witnessing and getting their friends saved. They were bringing their friends with them to church and sitting on the front row. I was witnessing this dynamic change right before my very eyes. They were enjoying God, enjoying Jesus, enjoying being saved, and they were happy.

Christmas of 1972 ushered in a whole new life experience. I invited Kirk and Alan to come live with me, and they became my roommates—Alan was my secretary's son, and he was a bearded, long-haired guy who was also spirit-filled. Alan had never even been out of California, and since I had not been home for a couple of years, I took them both home with me to El Reno, Oklahoma during Christmas break.

While in Oklahoma, I and my roommates went by to see an old football buddy, Dale Holland and his wife—Dale was one of the guys that had received the Lord back at Central State, and who was getting others on that team saved. We were sitting at the table, and Dale began telling me that he and his wife Linda started attending his wife's uncle's spirit-filled, charismatic church. I just kind of flinched. He looked straight at me and said, "I speak in tongues now, Paul." In my mind, I was thinking, "Oh, God." I could hear my two friends, and out of the corner of my eye I could see them all excited and giving each other high fives.

Then Dale started witnessing to me about the baptism. For a year I had been trying to run from it, and I looked at him and said, "Dale, I believe that tongues are okay for some people but not for everybody." As soon as the words left my lips, I knew that was the biggest copout in the world. I didn't know whether he was going to believe the line or keep pushing, but he graciously backed off.

We had a good visit, and later that night we went back to my parent's house. I had a lot going through my mind, but I was mainly thinking about the difference in Dale. We had known each other since junior high, and I could tell something was not the same about him. My spirit was screaming, "You nut; this is what you need; this is what you prayed for. This is what you asked God about."

I finally told the guys, "Guys, I need it, I need it. Would you lay hands on me?" Kirk was on one end of the couch and I was on the other with a pillow between us. He grabbed the pillow, flipped it onto the floor, and said, "Get on your knees." I got down on my knees, the two of them laid hands on me and prayed, and something happened inside of me. I didn't speak in tongues until sometime later, but a peace came over me and in me, and I knew at that moment everything was going to be ok.

The next night we went to a youth club there in El Reno. It had two sets of double doors; we went through one set of doors, and as we were getting ready to go through the second set, the anointing fell on us. We stopped. It arrested us. We looked at one another. Our eyeballs were bulging. We looked at each other

34

and asked, "Do you feel that?" When we got inside we knew why. This was supposed to be a Christian coffee house, but it was anything but that. The coffee house was being sponsored by one of the churches in town, and their youth pastor was running it. But that person was very liberal—actually I questioned whether she was even saved to tell you the truth. We pulled the plug on the jukebox and began to preach. That night about nine kids got saved. *I had never felt such power.* An anointing—a boldness— came on me like I had never felt in my entire life.

Christmas break came to an end, and we returned to San Diego in January of '73. The whole time we were driving back to San Diego, I was thinking, "What am I going to do? What has happened to me?" In my mind I knew that I had changed, and I knew that I was different, but I wasn't sure what had happened. What? How? God began to lead me to some really spirit-filled meetings, and it was as if a whole new world opened up to me under the power and anointing of God that I didn't even know existed.

I resigned as youth pastor in late 1973. God led both Kirk and I back to El Reno, where we eventually started a coffee house type ministry.

Several months after returning to Oklahoma, we made plans to return to San Diego for a Morris Cerullo meeting, but we didn't have the money to go to San Diego. By this time Kirk's brother, Mark, was

35

living with us, along with my brother, Curtis. Despite the fact we couldn't afford to make the trip, and we didn't know where the money was going to come from, we made plans to go to California and stay with Kirk's parents.

At midnight, a young friend of ours I had known in high school and with whom we had been working, stopped by to talk to us about something. As he was leaving, he stopped, turned around, and he said, "Oh, I forgot something. Man, I have wanted to give this to you guys for weeks, but I keep forgetting." He then handed us a whole pile of money. It was around two hundred dollars and exactly the amount that we had figured we needed for gas and everything to get us back to San Diego. We had made our plans by faith, and the answer came to us at midnight, six hours before we were planning to leave. God had provided a way, and we went to those wonderful meetings, marveling at the way God had blessed us.

While in San Diego, Kirk introduced me to a sweet young lady and her daughter who both came back with us as we returned to Oklahoma. Our goal was to do a Jesus House ministry like they had done in San Diego. (The concept just didn't take hold and by 1975 Kirk had moved back to San Diego.)

The more that I was around the young lady and her daughter, the more I thought that maybe she was to be my wife, and I could be a daddy to the little girl with whom I had fallen in love. This child was the most precious beautiful little girl. I not only became like a daddy to the child, but also became physically intimate with her mother. I found myself somewhere I thought I would never be. Ignoring my calling to the ministry and my witness for God, I had sex with a woman who was not my wife, and in the process she gave birth to my only son.

King David, after being confronted about his sinful behavior with Bathsheba, wrote in Psalm 51, "Have mercy on me O God...against thee, and thee only, have I sinned and done this evil in thy sight." After my inexcusable behavior and allowing myself to surrender to fleshly desires, I understood the depths of David's prayer. I had not only sinned against God, I had fathered a son with someone to whom I was not married. I was certain I had destroyed everything around me and had deeply hurt many who had looked up to me. What I did was wrong, and I would have to suffer the consequences. T.L. Osborn once said, "Sin will take you farther than you want to go; keep you longer than you want to stay; and cost you more than you want to pay." Such was my story.

I discovered that the woman I was intimate with was still married, and marriage was out of the question. I couldn't stand myself for what I had done, but I think I was even more upset by how I had failed God.

There were big grain elevators by the house where our ministry was located, and the railroad tracks ran right by them. So, at night, sometimes I would go and sit on the concrete platform just above the railroad tracks crying and pleading to God.

I had greatly sinned against God, and I believed that I would never have the wife, family, or the home that God had intended me to have. I also was certain that I could never be what God had called me to be. I also believed that I would never have the ministry or the church that God had intended for me. I truly felt that I had blown it. I was sitting above those railroad tracks just crying and begging God for mercy and forgiveness. I felt like I had asked Him to forgive me ten zillion times. I didn't know what to do about a mother with two children—one of them my very own son. Guilt plagued my soul. Marriage was not an option, yet I loved the little girl, and I had a four-month-old son by this time, and oh, how I didn't want to abandon him or her.

I sat above those railroad tracks and weeping and crying so much until I didn't have any tears left. I was just "teared out." Then, suddenly, down in my spirit, like one of those tiny flashlights, there was this little light of hope. That's the way to describe it. I use the word "hope" because that is what it was—not a world's wishing hope, but a biblical, favorable, confident expectation hope of the future. Somewhere down in my soul, God let me know that everything was going to be okay.

I—all of us—were going to be okay. In the darkness, in the ugliness, in the hurt, in the pain, and in the agony, a little spark of hope rose up in me that I was able to hang on to. And, out of that I felt His love and I knew that He loved me. I sat there, my feet dangling above the railroad tracks, and I sang a song that I sang as a child, "Yes, Jesus loves me, yes, Jesus loves me, yes Jesus loves me, the Bible tells me so." And tears came again. For the first time I sang that song knowing the true meaning of it. Even in my darkest and worst time, He still loved me. When I had let Him down and failed Him the most, His Love broke through my pain and my hurt, and I knew I was going to be okay, and I knew the children would be okay. The road ahead was going to be a rough road, but I knew we were going to be okay. Deep in my soul God confirmed that one day I would again be a father to my son.

God began ministering to me and assured me that, "You are going to reap what you have sown," but He said, "I will get you through it. Everything is going to be okay."

Late in 1976, weeks later, I took the children and their mother to her mother and their grandmother in San Diego. I got them to a place where she and the kids would be okay and would be taken care of.

God has chosen to put the pieces together in a miraculous way. Today I have a relationship with my son I wouldn't trade for all the riches of this world. I made some tough choices, but God always has the ability to make our tough choices works of miraculous art.

Reflections from Paul

There are some truths about God that you should know.

If and when you reach a place in your life that you are spiritually unhappy and not satisfied with your spiritual experience, know that God is ready and able to take you to the next level.

He will always meet you at your level of faith. When you make the choice to go "deeper" with God, then there is one place that he will take you. It's the one place he provided for us on the day of Pentecost and that is, being filled with His Holy Spirit. He doesn't have a Baptist door or a Methodist door or a different experience for everyone. It's the same experience for all of us. It is Himself filling us with His glory and power. You will never regret doing this.

The other thing is, that no matter how badly you might have blown it or how hard you may have fallen, you can never fall out of the reach of God's mercy and forgiveness. When you read God's Word, you find that everyone who ever cried out to God for mercy found mercy.

On the cross, He carried my guilt and shame. He became what I was so I could become what He is.

If you have done some things in this life that you're ashamed of, you can know God's great love and forgiveness. First John 1:9 is written to Christians. It says, "If we confess our sins, he is faithful and just to forgive us our sins, and to cleanse us from all unrighteousness." All we have to do is go to Him and ask Him to forgive us. He's ready and willing. I think the hardest thing for us is to forgive ourselves. Forgive, however, we must.

In order to go on and become what God wants for us we cannot live with a constant sense of guilt hanging over our heads. That is the devil working overtime on our mind. God has thrown our sin into the sea of forgetfulness, never to be remembered again. I had to forgive myself and go on with my life. To do anything less than that was to say that God's forgiveness was not enough.

Because of God's great love and forgiveness, I have gone on to experience a wonderful fulfilled life of ministry as the pastor that God called me to be. I have been able to raise my son, who came to live with us when he was 11 years old. He is now in his 30's and in the ministry himself. We are now grandparents, for the fifth time. Know this: God gives back to us the life the devil tries to steal.

On the Road to Rhema – The Scenic Route

Thy Word is a Lamp unto My feet and a light unto my path...In all thy ways acknowledge Him, and He shall direct thy paths (Ps 119:105; Prv 3:6).

Sam's Story February, 1977

"Can you leave all this?" That was the question God placed on my heart in September of 1976. In February of 1977, I would face that question one final time. Ray wanted a divorce—again.

I had just returned from what I thought was a well-deserved vacation that Ray had told me I could take and then changed his mind about at the last minute. He was still angry that I went anyway. To resolve the issue and his anger, he told me he wanted a divorce. I responded, "You are always changing your mind, so I am giving you three days. I'm tired of moving back and forth." Every time I left, I was never able to take furniture or personal items. He would usually throw all my personal things out.

Ray stood firm, "No, I have really thought about it while you were gone. I want a divorce."

My response was equally firm. "None the less, I'm giving you three days." With those words I went to

43

take a bath and relax with my Phillips translation of the Bible in hand. While opening my Bible, I asked God, "What about that? Is this it? Is this the final time Lord?" I looked at where I had opened the Scriptures, and my eyes fell on 2 Corinthians 6:17 where the Apostle Paul instructed the Christians at Corinth to come out from among unclean people and be separate. The Lord spoke to me and said, "Come out from unclean people. I am separating you." Then my eyes fell on 6:14 where God asks, "What fellowship does darkness have with light?" I knew immediately that this was it—the end of the marriage. God was working to separate me from a life of filth and flesh that is mentioned in 2 Corinthians 7:1, which says we are to cleanse ourselves from filthiness of the flesh. I knew I would never again have to endure the sometimes physically, verbally and mentally abusive relationship. At that point I knew that I knew that I knew that God was preparing me for a new beginning.

Now, however, I had given Ray three days to change his mind. I reminded God and myself about those three days. I felt deeply that I had to honor my word. As soon as I finished with my bath, I went back to Ray and repeated my words: "Ray, if you haven't changed your mind on the third day, this will be the last time. I will not come back again. You need to think long and hard on this."

On the third day, I went to his office. "This is the third day. What decision have you made?"

"I have really thought about it, and I want a divorce." he said.

I replied, "When I walk out that door, that's the end of it; I will not come back!"

Ray again said, "Oh, you know you'll come back. You always do."

"No." I responded with God-given confidence and boldness, "Not this time!" I left the office, went to the house and started packing. This time I was determined to take my possessions with me. During the process of packing, an alarm went off in me. I kept rebuking it, thinking it was fear. I didn't realize God was speaking to my spirit, warning me to get out of the house. Ray had changed his mind.

He came in and wanted to work things out and was trying to maneuver me into the bedroom. I knew that I didn't dare allow that to happen, or I would wind up getting physically injured if I did not agree to go.

"It's over Ray. I will not come back." As unobtrusively as I could, I made my way outside. We lived across the street from a high school. I knew that if I could get around people, Ray would not make a scene.

Through the years, I had figured out ways to escape the house if he came home drunk or angry or seemed in any way ready to pick a fight with me. I always laid my keys down a certain way, arranged in a way that I could pick them up without making noise. I parked my car so that I could get it out of the garage

45

quickly, and often I parked my car outside the garage so I could make a quick getaway.

This day, however, I couldn't seem to find my keys, so I just moved as quickly as I could to be around the high school kids as they were getting out of school. Appearance was extremely important to Ray, and I knew that he would not do anything in front of the teenagers. He followed me to the school and sat down on the bench with me and tried to talk me into coming back. After awhile, realizing that I was serious, he got angry and huffed off and went back to the house, locking the door behind him.

Thankfully, I had parked my car outside and I realized I did have my car keys. I left and went to a friend's house. Later that evening the police escorted me back to the house to get a few clothes and makeup. That was the total of my assets—from almost a million dollars in real estate holdings and a wonderful home, to only a car, a few clothes, and some makeup.

(While in Seattle, I had received a phone call from Ray and was told that he had skipped the country and that if I wanted anything I had to go down and get it. It seems that he had lost a great deal of money that had been given to him by men associated with the mafia.

When I arrived back home, anything of real value had been sold and many of my personal items had been thrown away. What little was left I sold to pay creditors.)

"Could I leave it all?" Gladly. The Apostle Paul could not have expressed my heart's desire more clearly: "Forgetting those things which are behind...I press toward the mark for the prize of the high calling of God in Christ Jesus" (Phil 3:13-14). *I was grateful to be freed from a life of material possessions with a price-tag far beyond their value.* It was then I remembered the last two verses of 2 Corinthians 6: "And I will receive you, and will be a Father unto you and ye shall be my...daughter, saith the Lord Almighty."—Almighty Indeed!

Reflections from Samantha

After I left Ray, I received a good deal of questioning by well meaning Christians not wanting to see me get off track spiritually. I appreciated the concern, but, because of how the Lord had spoken to me and because of Ray's own history of adultery I knew I was on safe ground.

There are many, however, who do not feel like they are on "safe ground" to leave a spouse. No one can unequivocally tell you it is ok for you to leave a spouse. You have to know that God has spoken to you to leave.

When children are involved and physical abuse is involved, without question, a spouse needs to leave with the children. Statistically, when children grow up in a home that has physical and or verbal abuse, the children will grow up marrying abusive spouses or to be the abuser. Not only do you have an obligation legally to not put your children in such situations, you also have a spiritual obligation to protect your children to raise your children in a safe environment.

While this is not meant to be an exhaustive book on marriage and divorce, for those of you who are struggling with whether to leave a difficult marriage consider the following.

First Corinthians 7:12-13 states, "...if he/she BE PLEASED to dwell with him/her, let him/her not leave..." The Greek has the sense of "if he/she be pleased to walk *in accord or agreement or unity* with you." Does that spouse live in agreement and unity with the direction your life is taking? Is that unbelieving spouse living in peace with you or is there constant turmoil, even violence? If so, that spouse is not "pleased to dwell with you," and in such cases you are not under obligation to continue that relationship.

"Oh, but sister," I can almost hear some saying, "I'm married to a Christian who is violent and says I have to submit." Most of the time, violence is coming from the male partner, and they seem to all know the scripture in Ephesians 5:21..."Wives submit yourselves unto your own husbands, as unto the Lord."

You need to look at that scripture in light of what is above it. Verse 20 states, "Submitting *yourselves* one to another in the fear of God." The subject of that whole passage is submitting ourselves one to another. That "Christian" spouse has missed the whole message of that passage. There is an "honoring" of each other, not just, "Hey, I'm the high mucky muck around here! Bow down and obey me!" No, he/she is not honoring Christ by being violent. That "Christian" male spouse needs to read on to verse 25, which states, "Husbands, love your wives, even as Christ loved the church AND gave himself for it." There is a deeper requirement of the husband in a Christian marriage. That is to sacrifice his life, his wants, and his desires to honor and love his wife in the same way that Christ loved and gave His life for the Church.

Having said that about men, women have the same obligation to love their spouses and to treat them with dignity and honor. There is no place in a Christian marriage, for a women to be physically or verbally abusive to her spouse.

Several years after I left Ray and was in my second year at Rhema, I attended a conference. Dr. Kenneth Stewart, who was the Dean of Rhema at the time had written a book, titled, <u>Marriage, Divorce and</u>

Remarriage, that ministered on the subject and it opened a door of freedom for men and women everywhere who were held spiritual hostage by the teachings in their churches.

Men and women who were divorced were—and are—treated very badly by the Christian world because of a lack of understanding of this subject. They were good enough to sit in church and tithe but not good enough to work in the church. Pastors were kicked out of their churches because they were divorced. Never mind that the spouse had committed adultery or had left to go his or her own way. That attitude has left many churches but does still exist in some circles. I encourage you to get that book, if it is still in print. There is another more current book, written by Kenneth E. Hagin, also titled, "Marriage Divorce and Remarriage." Either of those books will help you tremendously if you are struggling with those issues.

Reflections from Paul

I think one of the injustices we have done to the teaching of submission, especially with women is this: Men have abused this so terribly. Anytime that someone is making you submit, it is no longer submission, it is subjection. Submission is only something that you can do to yourself. It is voluntary.

Just because we are the male species does not mean that automatically we are better and that women are a cheaper, less important creation. As a matter of fact, basically the job description that God has for us as husbands means more responsibility. He requires more of us as husbands. In laying down our lives and loving them as Christ loved the Church, we are required to give our lives for them. We're also instructed to dwell with them with understanding, giving honor to them. That is an awesome responsibility.

I often ask men, "What has great value to you? How do you treat those things; your tools, your truck, your fishing equipment? The things we give honor to are the things that have value to us." They usually say, "Well I treat them differently."

Ephesians 5:22 says that wives are to submit to their own husbands, but you will also note in the scripture above it states we are to submit to one another. We cannot take the one scripture out of context of verses 21-25. Wives, note not all women are to submit to all men, wives are to submit to their own husbands. Nothing in those scriptures mean because I am the male I am better. It simply means that God has a higher job calling on me. There is more responsibility as the husband, "to love her as Christ loved the Church and gave himself for it, washing her with the water of the Word..."

For years I have listened to couples as they sit with me for counseling. The husband often says, "I'm the man, tell her to submit to me." Always, the husband wants her to submit, quoting that particular scripture but never wanting to admit to the scriptures surrounding it. They don't want to obey God's Word but they sure expect their wives to.

Honor has with it the understanding of value, importance or respect. It is our job as husbands to honor, value and respect our wives according to 1st Peter 3:7. My wife should not have to ask or demand that I give her honor. It is my place and responsibility to give it. I am responsible to see her through the eyes of Christ.

He saw something of value in us that He considered His life worth giving for. He asks us as husbands to do the same.

Sam's Story 1977-1983

The marriage was over, and I was on my way to a new beginning. That night I went to a friend's house. Vi, or Violet, was the mother of the pastor of a church that I had attended. He had since moved to Seattle.

After being escorted by the police to my home and picking up a few clothes and some makeup, I returned to Vi's home and stayed with her for two weeks. One thing I was grateful for was that two weeks before we separated, Ray had given me the cash to pay off my car, and I had the pink slip in my purse. I realized later it was just part of God going before me and preparing a way of escape. We waited for the pastor of the church I had been attending to return—I had been told by some of the members of the church that I needed the pastor's permission to leave. The pastor finally returned and seemed to be surprised that I thought I needed his permission. When I discovered that wasn't true, and I had a green light to leave, I was gone.

I drove through the night. I no longer had credit cards, but I did have a little cash—but virtually little else. On the way I ran into a heavy fog that had

53

traffic moving at a snail's pace, so I stopped at a rest stop in Ashland, Oregon, located just south of Medford, and splashed my face with cold water. I came out of the restroom and there was a man leaning against a tree near the car. He startled me when he asked, "Where are you headed?" I told him and he said, "Follow me and I'll get you there safely."

The man got into a semi-truck, and I followed him for five hours as far as Portland, Oregon. In Portland, the fog suddenly lifted, and the truck just as suddenly disappeared. I realized that two miracles had transpired that night—the first being that I drove for five hours and never had to fill my gas tank and two, when the truck disappeared in front of me, I realized God had sent an angel to get me safely through the fog.

I saw that I needed gas and thought I would get over the state line into Vancouver, Washington, and stop for gas. It was about 2:00 a.m., and to my dismay all the gas stations were closed. I tried calling the road service agency I had, but they would not come out and help me get gas. Frustrated and tired, I parked the car on a side street next to a gas station.

I was awakened at about 5:00 a.m. by a knock on my car window. I rolled down my window and a police officer asked if he could be of assistance. I explained my situation, so he took me to the gas station and filled my tank. I paid him and was on my way again. That tank of gas got me the rest of the way to Seattle—to me that was another miracle and that police officer was an angel.

I stayed in Seattle until October of 1979. I went from having a four bedroom, beautifully furnished home, and financially plush to sleeping on the floor in a trailer and living with 13 other people—but, I was happy being there and loved being with them. They provided me a safe haven from my husband who had guessed where I had gone and was still trying to get me to come back.

Through the years I had formed an opinion for some reason that a person couldn't get married a third time. I had forgotten the vision that I had had in early 1972. I don't know where I had gotten the idea that somehow you only got two chances at marriage. The desire to be married again was still very strong, and I prayed and asked God to take away this desire to be married. I was convinced that I had to stay single the rest of my life. So finally, I went to Bob, the Associate Pastor in Seattle, crying saying, "I just want to do what God wants!" All the while I'm thinking God wants me to be single.

He said, "Well, did you pray about this?"

In between sniffling and crying, I said, "Yes, I prayed for God to take it away."

I don't know what he called me—dork, silly, stupid or something. He laughed and said, "If you still have the desire that could only mean one thing. Do you think that God listens to your prayers?" I nodded my head yes, and he said, "He must want you married again." Boy, that was a new thought for me. It had never occurred to me that He would want me to be married for a third time. So, I began to ponder the thought of marriage, this time the right way: the right man, a Godly man, and forever.

I didn't know at that time that God was calling me into ministry. I had started attending some Toast Mistress Club meetings. At one of the workshops I attended, there was a woman who was teaching on self-image. I remember looking at her and telling God, "Lord, I would love to be able to minister to people like that." I didn't realize at the time that God was building that desire in me to be a minister. I wasn't sure women could minister and especially me, because of my past.

In October of 1979, I got a phone call from Vi, my pastor's mother. She had moved back to Oklahoma and needed someone to come and help with her restaurant while she had surgery. I was single with no encumbrances, so I decided I would go help her. The Lord had instructed me to sow my car into the ministry in Seattle, so I no longer had a car. I packed my meager belongings and boarded a bus for Vian, Oklahoma.

The long trip to Oklahoma gave me plenty of time to ponder many questions I had been asking God. I thought over things like, if the Bible says, "By His stripes you were healed," then why are we sick all the time? When I was in Seattle, it seemed like I was just sickly, always fighting flu or allergy symptoms. Everybody I knew at one point or another seemed to be sick with something. We would pray, but none of us ever seemed to get healed of anything.

Having just lost everything, another question I pondered was, "Does God just meet our needs? Is it God's will for some people to be poor and others to be rich? Why do Christians always seem to be at the mercy of the devil? The Bible says we have been given power over him so why do we always seem to be afraid of him? Then there was the question of women in ministry. Are women called to minister? What about those difficult passages of the Apostle Paul's in the Bible about women being silent in the church? There were so many questions and no answers. Yet, as I traveled through the days and nights on the bus, God had already gone ahead of me to answer all those seemingly unanswerable questions.

Arriving in Vian, Oklahoma, I got reacquainted with young Frank Long, Vi's son, now a junior in high school. He had been twelve years old when I met him at his brother's church. He would tag along with me everywhere I went, helping me with my rental houses or just in general being a fun pest. He was very dear to me.

Now in Vian, he was going to a little community church out in the middle of nowhere on a dirt road next to a cemetery. I remember the first Sunday that I went. The pastor was Patrick Bowen, who had just graduated from Rhema. Every service I went to was like water in the desert. At every service, question after question that I had been asking God would be answered. My previous pastors taught me obedience and unconditional love for people in spite of what they did. They had taught me a love for the Word of God. They had laid a foundation in me. Now, I was being prepared for another step in my future. God was inexorably taking me to my destiny.

Patrick ministered to me in many ways during that period in Vian concerning the husband that was in my future and things having to do with ministry. He had given me a book that I still have today, God's Word to Women by Kathryn Bushnell. It answered all those difficult questions that I had about women in ministry.

With everything I had been taught by my pastors on the West coast and armed with all that Patrick had taught me in Oklahoma, I thought I was going back to the West coast. I had finally accepted that I was indeed called to ministry. I thought I would go back to Oregon, where I grew up, and start a little

Bible study. In my heart I felt like I had all this wonderful knowledge and it was important for me not to keep it to myself, but share it with others. So I started packing to go back to Oregon.

God had other plans in mind. By the spring of 1980, I realized that I wasn't going back to Seattle. I was somewhat disappointed, but still excited. It was April of 1980. I remember the night well. It was Oklahoma hot, the hottest one on record at that time! The air conditioner wasn't working. There were guest ministers, graduates of Rhema, who had come down to minister for Patrick. One of the women ministered to me saying, "Don't go too soon. If you go too soon, you will miss the plan of God. It will take much longer for God to do what He intends to do for you." This is the paraphrased basic message—don't leave. I wasn't pleased. I didn't want to be in Oklahoma, but I knew in my heart she was right.

My mind went back to when I first arrived in Oklahoma. I had been in Vian about a month when my mother called crying. Immediately, I thought something was wrong with my dad or one of my siblings. Alarmed, I asked, "Mom! What's wrong?" She cried out, "I just don't want you to marry an Okie!" That caught me off guard. I looked at my phone, wondering if I had heard her right. She repeated it, and I assured her immediately, laughing, "Mom! It's

OK! I'm only here for another month. I'm not going to marry an Okie!"

In my spirit, I heard the words, "Don't say that!" Somehow I knew I would marry an Okie, but I didn't know enough at the time to take it to heart, so I pushed it to the back of my mind until that hot, eventful night when everything changed for me.

I stayed in Vian that spring and summer, praying about what to do. The pastor took some church members and me to Rhema to hear a guest speaker. We went to Prayer and Healing School that afternoon. After the service I went to a counselor, talking to her about all my struggles and frustrations and wondering what to do with my life and why I was in Oklahoma. She very gently said to me, "Samantha, you need to very seriously consider Rhema!" Well, that was another new thought to me. Never in a million years would I have thought that God would allow this little mountain girl to go to such a wonderful place as Rhema. I was overwhelmed.

After much prayer I finally realized that God was telling me to go to Rhema. That posed another whole set of challenges for me. I still didn't have very many clothes. Actually, I didn't even own a dress. Remember, when I left California I had only what I had been allowed by the police to grab from my home in just a few minutes.

Now, I was headed to ministry school, with no clothing suitable for the dress requirements, no money for tuition, no job, and no car. The Lord had not allowed me to take a paying job while in Seattle and He would not allow me to take a salary from Violet when I was in Vian. So I had worked for nearly three years without a salary. I didn't realize at the time that I was sowing seed for my future.

Patrick filled out my pastoral recommendation, and I was accepted. I was on my way to Rhema Bible Training Center in Broken Arrow, Oklahoma!

Reflections from Samantha

I learned a lot of life lessons during my time in Seattle and Vian. The most important of those lessons were that God loved me and He had my best interest at heart. There were times when I would feel all alone and with no sense of direction. Sometimes I would wake up in the middle of the night crying. At those times I would always turn to God and to the Bible for direction.

One night I was feeling particularly abandoned and felt impressed to open my Bible and begin reading. I opened it to Isaiah 54. The very first words on the page grabbed my attention. "Sing O barren, thou that didst not bear; break forth into singing, and cry aloud, thou that didst not travail with child: for more are the children of the desolate than the children of the married wife, saith the Lord." I had never been able to have children and I've left a husband who certainly did not have my best interests at heart. I realized God was telling me something in that verse but I wasn't sure what.

As I read the rest of the chapter, I was reminded again that God had plans for my life. I knew that I wasn't abandoned. Here in the midnight hour God was giving me hope for a future. What that future was at the time I didn't know. But I did know God. I had watched Him repeatedly protect, encourage, and strengthen me. There were times when I felt like I couldn't take one more step, and I would open my Bible, and God would show up through His Word and tell me I could make it. I could then take one step more than I thought I could. That night as I lay on the floor on the two pillows that constituted my bed, I finished reading Isaiah 54. I knew again that God was preparing a wonderful future for me. All He was asking me to do was believe Him, take Him at His Word and watch Him perform His Word for me.

So I am saying to you that no matter what the crisis is in your life; no matter how desperate things seem to be, turn to the Lord for direction. He knows you by name and cares for you more than you will ever comprehend. He has a wonderful plan—a destiny for your life. Jeremiah 29:11 NIV says, "For I know the plans I have for you, declares the Lord. Plans to prosper you and not to harm you, plans to give you hope and a future."

God has a plan for your future no matter how dark it may look right now. The Lord had to teach me to follow Him a step at a time. So many times we want everything planned out for the next 20 years, but God doesn't always do that. Usually it is step by step. He tells you the first step, you take it and then, direction comes for the next step.

In those days I didn't know how to tap into God's future for my life. All I knew was to take whatever step was before me at that point. I never in a million years would have moved to Oklahoma voluntarily. I just knew my friend, Vi, needed help and I was available, so I volunteered. Yet...there was a plan being fulfilled. God had a plan. I didn't know at the time that He was putting me in the ministry. Me? In the ministry? Wow! What an awesome plan. I wouldn't have put me there, yet God saw something in me that I didn't see. I didn't know there was a wonderful hunk of a husband waiting for me. That scripture about more would be the children of the desolate one...I'm a pastor's wife! I have all kinds of spiritual children. I didn't know that at the time. I knew it was a promise of the Lord and that I was to hang on to it, and I knew I was to follow each step as

He gave it to me. Little by little He brought each piece of the plan together until it made a whole.

What does He see in you? Put your life in His hands. Put Him first. Put the Word of God first. James 1:5 says, "If any man lack wisdom, let him ask of God, that giveth to all men liberally and upbraideth not; and it shall be given him." Ask Him, He'll lead you...step by step...and He will never disappoint you. It will always be more wonderful than anything you plan for yourself.

Reflections from Paul

A girl in my youth group in San Diego gave me a little plaque that stated, "God will not guide you where He cannot provide for you." This little phrase always blessed me, as I would read it hanging on my wall. I had no idea the significance of it until later in my life and Sam's as God provided. He always provided for us as He guided us through to the ultimate destination of marriage and through all the years since.

I grew up Baptist and was taught that women could not be ministers. If that was God's intention then why is He giving so many women not only the desire to minister, but the anointing to minister? After I was filled with the Holy Ghost, three of the times that I considered to be the most important times of personal ministry to me were by women. God used them to bless me greatly.

On the Road to Rhema Via the Potter's Wheel

Forgetting those things which are behind, I press forward...

Paul's Story 1977-1982

A new beginning allows us to leave the past behind and to start on a fresh page in our journey with God. But a new beginning also means a time of allowing God to minister to us and mold us as well as a time of healing and restoration. The days and years following closing that chapter in my life where I failed God and myself were years of rediscovering my intimate relationship with God and a time of discovering God's plans and purpose for my life. The next several years God, the Master Potter, would place me on the potter's wheel to mold me, reform me, and fashion me according to His Divine Plan. What a joy to experience the cleansing forgiveness of God and what a thrill to be on the road again fulfilling God's calling and anointing on my life.

My son, James, was born in August of 1976, and in December of that same year, I took him, his half sister, and his mom back to California to her mother. I got them settled in, but I had a really hard time leaving my son. I remember that I just broke down crying. It was one of the hardest days of my life. Kirk picked me up and took me to Jim Roche's where I stayed for a couple of weeks. I had a distinct impression that I needed to stay, but I also had an impression that I should get back to Oklahoma and start taking care of everything that I had made such a mess of. Everybody was really upset with me back home, and I needed to get home and start clearing things up.

Struggling over when to leave, I finally picked a day and left. Before I left, I said goodbye to my son's mother, her daughter and my six-month-old son. Kirk picked me up and as I sat in Kirk's car, I began crying so hard that nothing was coming out. I don't think I had ever gone through such an emotional drain in my life. Kirk took me to wherever my car was—I think it was at the Jordan's for some reason.

Very early the next morning I left. I got about 80 miles out of San Diego up in the mountains before it drops down into the desert region. It was about lunchtime so I pulled into a rest stop and ate the lunch that Sue Jordan had fixed for me. After I finished eating, I tried to start the car and it wouldn't start. It was dead. There was nothing. I was thinking that was unusual, so I checked the battery, and found there was plenty of spark. Next, I wondered if it was the starter. I jacked up the car and crawled under, dropping the starter to see if maybe it was bad. I jumped the starter straight from the battery and it turned over. So, now I surmised that it was in the wiring somewhere between the battery and the starter. The fact was that the car would not start and I was stranded.

I sat there and began to sense the presence of God, so I started praying. During my time of prayer, I had a sense that I had to go back. I wasn't supposed to leave yet. I wrestled with that decision but finally said, "Okay, God, I'll go back to the Jordans, and I will stay until I know whatever it is You are trying to tell me or are wanting me to do." I reached up, hit the ignition and it started right up. It kicked right off! I left the roadside park and headed back. Jim had told me that I was welcome to stay there as long as it took, so I stayed with him. The next week I was able to get a part-time job with the Morris Cerullo Ministry.

Shortly after I returned, I was invited to dinner at the Jordan's. While I was having dinner, a good friend of mine, Craig Stanley, came walking through the door, saw me, and got all excited. He pointed at me and said, "Don't go anywhere!" He rushed out and came back through the door about fifteen minutes later with Willie Sheer, a local pastor and good friend. Willie said, "Man! God gave me a word for you. We thought that you were already gone." They took me back into the bedroom, and we all began praying. Willie began speaking to me about my life. I don't actually recall exactly the things he told me, but they had a healing effect on me, and through the years I'm certain all that he spoke has come to pass in my life.

During that time I went to various meetings. The first meeting I went to was at Willie's house. His house was full of people. He ministered and then began praying for people. He turned and looked at me and told me to come help him. I was afraid because I hadn't prayed for anybody in a long time. I didn't think I was worthy. I didn't think I could pray for anybody. I had put myself on a shelf because of my "mess." I thought God was still mad at me and that He was through with me, but Willie insisted I come up front with him. So I went up, and I got around back to catch people. Willie said, "No, no, I want you around here in front of them. I want you to pray for them." There was a young lady in the group that I started praying for, and God started showing me very clearly some things that were going on with her. I realized that some of the gifts of the Spirit were working in me. In my mind, I'm saying, "God, I don't deserve this." And basically, He said, "Yeah, you're right. You don't deserve this, but it doesn't have anything to do with you. It's all about her and what she needs. You are my gift right now, and I'm going to use you to help her." So I began sharing with her what the Lord showed me. I told her there was an older gentleman that had been trying to get her to move in with him. He had kids her age, and he had been tempting her. God had been trying to tell her, "No," and her parents had been telling her "No," but still, she had been seriously considering doing it. Her eyes got really big and she looked at Willie and everybody else. They were all saying, "We didn't tell him this. We didn't say anything to him." She was almost angry about it because she thought that everyone told me these things about her. I found out later that she didn't move in with the guy.

That was the beginning. They brought several other people up for me to pray with. Nobody was as excited as I was. I realized that the ministry was not over. For me, that night was the beginning of a new beginning, getting me back on track. It was like a weight left me.

Even though God had confirmed to me that everything was going to be okay back in Oklahoma when I was on the railroad tracks, I was still battling with ministry. At that time in Oklahoma, I didn't translate "everything is going to be okay" to include a restoration of my ministry. Not until that night at Willie's did I understand the full impact of God's promise.

God's restoration was in full blossom. I pondered on the events at Willie's home, and I remember asking myself if I still felt like my ministry was over? And out of me came the answer, "Did David stop being king?" The answer was for me, out of me. Out of my own spirit, God answered me. I realized then that even though David did everything that he did, he did not stop being king. Boom! It just boomed out of me. It wasn't something I thought up. It was the Spirit of God speaking through my spirit to me! At the time I was driving through Lemon Grove, California and realized what I had just said. I began crying, praising God, thanking God, and worshipping Him because all of the sudden I realized that it wasn't over for me! God wasn't done with me! I was back!

The time I spent in San Diego gave me time to work through some more things with my son's mom. I was actually able to leave in better shape with her. She wasn't happy about the way things had turned out, but after being there for a while, she was more able to accept some things. That afternoon on that mountain when God led me to return to San Diego was truly divine healing intervention. God's spiritual medical team was there in California not Oklahoma. I believe God knew what condition I was in. There was really no one in Oklahoma that could restore me that would love me, and would reach out and hang on to me like these three brothers in Christ did. They wouldn't let go of me. I was dragging my feet and they wouldn't let me. I am so grateful that they made me minister to people. I continued to go to meetings, and as I did I was getting more and more free. I realized, I was back on track and it was through the ministry of these dear friends.

The Jordan's were Presbyterian and a few weeks later they had their youth group—about 15 kids—come in order that I might minister to them. I ministered to them about the Baptism in the Holy Spirit. One boy stood up and said, "I want what you're talking about." I walked over to him, laid hands on him, and prayed for him. He exploded into speaking in tongues and praising God with tears streaming down his face. Then he turned and laid hands on the next kid. I only laid hands on maybe two more. They started laying hands on each other. The Spirit of God began moving throughout the room. Before it was all over, that whole house was full of the glory of God. Those kids were all filled with the Holy Ghost that night, praising, crying, and worshipping God.

God was blessing me by allowing me to bless others. My time with Jim, Willie, and Craig spent in prayer and fellowship was a wonderful, restorative, healing time for me.

Shortly after that I finally was able to leave again. This time was totally different. I was different. The car didn't stop on me. This time I knew. Yes, I knew it was time to go. The first time I just wanted to go home, but I wasn't ready.

It was early 1977, well on my way to recovery, the blessings of God on me, and on track. I returned to Oklahoma in better shape to deal with people. There were a lot of people who were hurt through what I had done, and I was able to apologize to them and begin the healing process with them. Through the years, many people in town still remembered, but now they marveled at the change that has transpired. For instance, the former Assembly of God pastor, his wife , and I were really good friends, and I continue to see them often. They have retired, and a year or two ago his wife said to me, "You know, we are very proud of you that you have recovered from all that stuff all those years ago and that you have gone on to become the man of God that you have." They had been very upset with me back then. I watched God restore many of those relationships through the years. You can really blow it and make a really big mess of things, but God can restore you. He can restore everything that Satan steals from you, I know. He's done it for me.

Shortly after returning home, my brothers, Curtis, Martin, and I started some Bible studies in Martin's home and in some other homes. The groups started growing. It was neat to see what God was doing.

Although things were going well in Oklahoma, God had different plans for my life. Within a few months after returning home, Willie Sheer called me and told me he was going back to Kentucky and the Lord had told him that I was supposed to come back to California and pastor his church, Trinity Temple. They had already gotten a place to meet. I was somewhat stunned and said something smart like, "What?" After much prayer, I realized it was time to go back to California.

I left the Bible studies in Martin and Curtis' hands. It was now close to summertime. Willie had left for Kentucky taking Craig Stanley with him. I became pastor of Trinity Temple. In that whole time there was more healing and more strengthening.

James was now about two years old. During that time I got to develop a relationship with him and his half sister who was about four years old.

In 1979, God released me from California, and I moved back to Oklahoma. As I returned, the Lord told me that the Bible study group's my brothers and I had started were going to become a church. By this time a pastor named Richard Angel from Oklahoma City was teaching the groups. My first night home I attended the Bible study. They were voting on whether or not to become a church. God had given me a supernatural dream in San Diego about this happening, and I sat there marveling, going "Wow!" I remember thinking, "Okay, am I supposed to be the pastor or is he the pastor?" As I prayed over the situation, asking God, "What's going on?" the Lord spoke to me that Richard was to become the pastor and that I was to help him. We moved into a storefront building in El Reno, and the church began to rapidly mushroom.

There was a big group of people driving from Mustang—about 20 miles away—attending the church. One Sunday afternoon we were introduced to each other, and something just clicked. Richard approached me and suggested that I go to Mustang and help them start a Bible study. So Curtis and I would drive to Mustang where we met in a lady's home. We had been working with that group for about two months when Richard took all of us to Rhema Bible Training Center to hear Hilton Sutton, a famous end-time speaker. While there, God spoke to my brother, Curtis, about enrolling at Rhema. This was the first time I knew anything about his plans and began thinking about what we were going to do without him. He was our music leader, and I needed him to help me. But those thoughts were fleeting as we gathered around him, praying for him and his plans for Bible school.

In the fall of 1980, Curtis went to Rhema. I stayed at the Bible study in Mustang. I didn't see Curtis much that entire school year. What I didn't know was that God had plans for me that also involved Rhema. In February of 1982, Curtis invited me to Rhema to hear Lester Sumrall, and during that time Curtis introduced me to his friend, Samantha.

Reflections from Paul

Second Chronicles 16:9 states, "For the eyes of the Lord run to and fro throughout the whole earth, to show himself strong in the behalf of them whose heart is perfect toward him....." That verse became a wonderful blessing in my life, especially in the days and years after my fall.

Life is not over just because you've made mistakes or sinned. God's plans for your life do not change. Romans 11:29 states that God's gifts and His call are irrevocable. When God ministered to me that David didn't stop being King, it brought such hope to me. It is true David had to go through some difficult times—he lost the son born out of his sin as well as several other things, but God got him through it. He was king for about 40 years and was "a man after God's own heart."

The book of Jeremiah 29:11 is another verse of promise that got me through some very dark times. "For I know the thoughts that I think toward you, saith the Lord, thoughts of peace, and not of evil, to give you an expected end." God knows the plans He has for you and they are always good. God has a way of taking hurting people and making them wonderful instruments of healing. Before I slipped up and fell, I had very little compassion for people who sinned.

After God restored me, I have a heart of love and understanding for those who have "blown it." I now understand His great, great love for us and that His love has no limits. The Lord spoke to me one time and said, "People do not understand or see the blood of Jesus as I do through My eyes. That blood cost Me a great price. In My eyes when I see it applied to My people, it puts a great value on them. It is the blood of My Son and it has great importance to Me."

Destination Rhema

And God Said, "Let the Romance Begin"

"Wherever you go, I will go...your people shall be my people, and your God, my God" Ruth 1:16

My younger brother went off to Rhema, and I wasn't sure what a RHEMA was or who Kenneth Hagin was. I had already read a book of his and had not put the two together. Curtis invited me to come up to hear Lester Sumrall at Winter Bible Seminar in February of 1982, so I went up on a Friday night. After the conference, my brother was introducing me to everyone, because he knew everybody. Then suddenly he stops and wheels around and I crashed into him. He was looking all serious and I said, "What?"

He said, "There's a lady over here and I want you to meet her. She and I sit together in some classes, and she is a really good friend."

I'm going yeah, yeah, yeah! I couldn't really care less. We were in what is now called Rooker Memorial Auditorium. So we walked over to the camera stand. There was a big crowd talking to her and then she turned and greeted Curtis. When I laid my eyes on her, I went, "Ahhhhh such a WOMAN!" My heart was going up in my throat and I'm telling myself, "BE STILL! COOL DOWN!" It turned out she had been looking for Curtis to see what "the group" was doing that evening. We made arrangements to meet at the local pizza place. Somewhere in the process, I found out how old she was and was very disappointed because she was quite a bit older than me. I really liked her, but because of past experience, I was concerned about that. I didn't want to chase her, and I didn't want to start anything that wasn't of God, so I kept my distance.

(Samantha) When I laid eyes on Paul, I thought, "Oh! Be still my heart! Such a HUNK!" I was trying to put a clamp on my singing heart and remind myself that he was 5 ½ years younger than me and that he had never been married. I had no intention of marrying someone younger than myself, but I still walked over to student housing, my feet barely touching the ground, and looked for the best thing I had to wear to make a really good impression.

(Paul): It was and it did!

(Samanthal): I'm home trying to act nonchalant and keep a silly grin off my face. I told my roommates that I was going out with Curtis and the gang and, oh yeah, his older brother Paul. While I was getting ready, a couple of my roommates came up to me and said, "Sam we really think we just heard God say this guy is your husband!"

I said, "No! No! He's too young for me...but at least he's in the ballpark and he is gorgeous!" Even now, all these years later I still love to just stare at him...what a Hunk! People need to understand that God is not going to put you with someone you don't like.

I spent that night trying to watch him without his realizing I was watching him.

(Paul): I was doing the same thing—looking all over for her; trying to watch her without her realizing it. We all went out again the following night and afterwards, we—Curtis and I—took several of the "gang" home. Kirk DuBois was with us, and the Spirit of God dropped on us, and we began to minister to several of them—including Samantha. The Lord had a word for her. I ministered to her that she needed to stop being afraid of men because she was holding back and not stepping on into ministry because she was afraid of men and their opinion and what they would think of a woman minister. Then the words came up in me to minister to her about her "secret desire."

So, very strongly, I began to speak a word to her from the Lord about her "secret desire." I knew in my heart that the secret desire was her husband, and that she would know and understand it was from God.

As I started ministering to her, deep down in my spirit the Lord said, "IT'S YOU!" I kept going, "NAH! NAH! It's not me," but the Lord kept saying, "NO, it's you!" I'm thinking to myself, "Paul, you're crazy, you're just trying to make this thing happen." It felt so silly; I probably cut short ministering to her because I didn't want to project something that might not be God.

(Samantha): He ministered to me and I knew that it was about my husband. I went home and wrote it all down.

After having met Paul, later on a bunch of us would get together and go down to "Curtie's" house to visit his Mom and Dad. Yeah! Right! I would go and try not to look like a total idiot just being around Paul. I kept trying to tell myself that he wasn't my husband and told myself all kinds of reasons why he wasn't. It never occured to me to ask the Lord.

Over the years God had been talking to me a lot about what my future husband was like—mostly about his personality and character. During my first year at Rhema, I remember driving home from work late one night seeing the beautiful homes I was driving past, and I began dreaming a little about what it would be like to meet his parents at the front door of one of those homes. I began thinking of what I would say and what he would say and how witty we would be...it was a great imagination. The Lord broke in on my reverie and said, very clearly, to me, "You'll like your husband; he's fun to be with!" It was a wonderful revelation to me. I didn't want a boring, quiet man. I wanted someone who was fun and who laughed a lot and enjoyed people. I laughed and began praising God and promptly went home and wrote it in my journal.

During the fall of my second year at Rhema, before I met Paul, I had walked in to what is now known as Rooker Memorial Auditorium. I was getting ready for a skit we were doing during "Share and Praise." Suddenly, I stopped and bent over, groaning, and saying, "Oh! God! Where is my husband?" I looked up and saw the camera stand in the middle of the auditorium. I turned and looked toward the south doors and immediately a peace came over me, the groaning stopped, and a sense of something having just taken place in my spirit swept over me. I didn't know what it was, but I knew something spiritual had happened.

In February, 1982, at the Winter Bible Seminar, Lester Sumrall was the guest speaker, and that Friday night I was free and went looking for Curtis, Paul's brother, after the service. I was at the camera stand, and I looked toward the south doors, and there was Curtis with Paul—my future husband—coming toward me. In April of that same year, I was getting ready to go minister in Vian. While blow drying my hair, I was thinking about my parents and one particular

Christmas. I'm the oldest of nine children and my parents always bought two gifts a piece for us since that's what they could afford. One Christmas they got a late check back from the IRS and they splurged on Christmas. We lived on a guest ranch and the guest house was where my parents hid the Christmas gifts. One night we kids sneaked over and tried to peer in the windows, but they had the blinds drawn. We could hear them giggling and laughing like little kids wrapping our gifts.

As I pondered that I started laughing. The Lord broke in and said, "I had fun shopping for your husband. You'll like him!" He reminded me of a message a friend of mine once told me that the Lord showed him about marriages. The Lord had said to him, "There are marriages I bless because I am asked to bless them, and I bless them as far as I am able." Then the Lord said to me, "Your marriage is one that I will bless because you have allowed Me to bring My very best for you."

That message from the Lord about marriage was very important to me because during my second year at Rhema, Curtis and a group of us ended up doing a lot of things together. One of those things was that we had all read Paul Yonghi Cho's book, The Fourth Dimension. It was a wonderful book and emphasized our need to define very specifically what we were believing God for. So all my young friends were making a list of what they wanted in a spouse. I got on the bandwagon and began to write down what I thought I wanted in a husband. I got about three sentences down and hit a blank wall. I stopped writing, trying to think of what to write. Then I realized, I couldn't write anything down. I had had two failed marriages, both out of the will of God.

It was vitally important to me that I not make a mistake again. I appealed to the Lord and prayed, "Lord, who am I kidding, I don't know what I need in a husband, much less what I want; but You know me. You know what makes me tick, You're the one who created me and You know what You've called me to. I trust You and I trust You to choose my husband for me. So You choose him and bring him to me." Now, these several months later, as I looked towards the south doors and saw Paul coming towards me, I realized God was verifying to me that He was indeed at work in my life.

During my two years as a student I lived with three young students who were around 19—20 years old. They were attractive, sharp young women and understandably, had lots of guys around. They would go out for a date, and at times I would be so lonely I would curl up in my bed and cry. One afternoon, as I was crying...again...the Lord spoke to me and said, "Samantha, turn that energy you're spending on crying and begin praying for your spouse. Whatever you're going through he's going through; so begin praying for him." So I did. I thought to myself, when I'm lonely, he must be lonely so I would pray I Corinthians 13 over him. I prayed for his finances; I prayed for purity—whatever I was going through, I would pray for my spouse, whoever he was.

Then the Lord said, "Plan your wedding, it will help you stay in the place of faith." When I realized God really did have a husband for me, I thought in terms of a small wedding, with a few close friends, but the Lord said, "No, you're going to have a large wedding and wear white." I sort of balked at that for awhile because of having been married twice before. Then the Lord spoke very clearly to me and said, "Samantha, if I have forgiven you, then as far as I am concerned, you have never been married before. You have been forgiven of your past. I don't know your past. You are fresh and clean to Me."

So I happily went out with my friend Leslie, exploring all the wedding shops around town. We had a great time dreaming and laughing and just being silly. Once, a sales girl asked me when the wedding was. That caught me up short for a minute. After all, I wasn't even engaged—didn't even know who the groom was! I immediately felt guilty, then, the Lord gave me a brilliant answer! Out of my mouth came the words, "We haven't set the date yet," which was true! So we continued blithely along, dreaming about

84

my wedding day, praying and believing God for His promises to me.

That spring I graduated from Rhema. The following August "the gang" celebrated one of the girl's birthday by going to the Pedestrian Park on the Arkansas River. There was a children's playground made up as a little Western Village and we sometimes went there and played around like ten-year-olds. We had a picnic that night at the park. At some point in the evening, Paul and I had struck up a conversation and we took a walk. We got within ten feet of one of the street lights and it went out. I just thought it had burned out but about ten feet past it, it went back on. We passed by another one and it did the same thing.

(Paul): I was looking at her teasing her and wondering what was going on. We looked to see other people walking under the lights, but they didn't go off. It only happened when we were under them.

(Samantha): It did that several times. I was thinking that it was the Glory of God manifesting but for an entirely different reason than what I realized later. We were talking about God and discussing scripture. I had especially been thinking about the glory of God at that time, so I attributed it to the fact that we were talking about the Lord and that He was just manifesting His presence in that way.

(Paul): Both of us had made so many mistakes with our lives that we were extremely cautious about getting involved with anyone. It had been about eight years since my son was born. During that time I had had maybe five to eight dates. I knew all those dates were a big NO! I knew that if I did anything, I'd just mess it up with her. By this time I had known Samantha about six months, and the only time I ever saw her was with the gang.

(Samantha): After graduating from Rhema in the spring of 1982, that following fall I traveled some, ministering in different churches and started my own cleaning/wallpapering business to supplement my income. I also was doing singles activities at Walnut Grove church. During that period God continued to tell me different things about my husband, and I would write them down.

(Paul): Sometimes people would say to me, "You're just afraid of marriage and commitment." I would say, "Yeah! That's true." I say to people now, "Don't rush, and don't let people pressure you into making a decision for marriage."

From time to time, I would drive up to see the gang. We'd go out to dinner and the movies. Sam and I played a sort of cat and mouse game with each other. I wanted to sit next to her, but I didn't want to send any wrong signals, plus I was so shell-shocked from bad relationships from my past and from making wrong decisions that I tried to stay away from her.

(Samantha): Curtis moved back to El Reno, and a couple of times we (mostly girls) would go down ostensibly to visit Curtis. I, on the other hand, was definitely more motivated that I would see Paul again.

Christmas season 1982 came around, and I didn't have the money to go home, and I didn't know where to spend Christmas. I didn't want to spend it alone, and I began to pray about it. I got a velvety feeling about going down to see Curtis and Paul and their family. On the night I was to drive down, I was on my way home to clean up and pack, and I got to thinking about boyfriends and girlfriends and for some reason I thought about carnivals. My brother, who is just younger than me would take a date to a circus or a carnival, and of course, they played all the carnival games. He would win all kinds of stuffed animals. Suddenly, I had an overwhelming desire for someone...not just anyone...but a man to care enough about me to buy me a stuffed animal. I had been married twice, and never had I been given a stuffed animal by someone who loved me. I arrived home and on the porch of my apartment was a package from my Mom and Dad. That in itself was unusual. Very seldom did my parents ever send me a package or letters, so receiving it was a special treat. I took the package up to my apartment and opened it and in it was a little pink stuffed cat with a red yarn bow around it. The kitty had long legs that would fold up under the front paws. I cried. I promptly named her Priscilla and sat her on my bed and left for El Reno.

Paul's parents never knew a stranger, and they welcomed me with open arms. I had a wonderful time, and on Christmas morning I opened up a Christmas gift that Paul gave me. In it was the cutest little over-stuffed Teddy Bear that had a little round tummy and a hairy chest and big strong arms! He reminded me of Paul. I promptly named him Chester...sort of to remind me of the fact that I wanted a man who had a hairy chest. The Lord reminded me of the scripture, "He gives us the desires of our heart." It blessed me that God cares so intimately about us.

(Paul): I had wanted to get her something that would remind her of me that wouldn't be too obvious. I was shopping downtown El Reno and in one of the local jewelry shops were these bears. When I saw this bear, I knew it was the one I wanted her to have.

(Samantha): I took it home with me and sat him beside Priscilla. Every time I looked at them together it would remind me to pray for my spouse. At the time I wondered whether Paul was my husband, but I would always dismiss it because he was younger than me and had never been married and had never been to Rhema. It was very important to me that the man God had for me have the same vision and understanding of the Word that I had received. For me that was someone who had been or was going to Rhema.

I went to El Reno a couple of times more but on the last trip I realized that those of us who were going down (we girls) were chasing Curtis and Paul. I had promised myself I wouldn't do that so I stopped going. In my heart I knew that God was bringing my husband to me and that I didn't have to chase anyone. That was in the early spring of 1983.

That summer, Rhema called and asked me to become the Student Life Activities Coordinator. God had told me to stay in the area, that He was opening a door for me to work there, so it was a joy when they called. I had to complete some jobs I had going on at the time, and one night I came back to my apartment so tired I just wanted to drop. As I headed up the stairs I remembered a fun thing that Curtis, Paul, and the gang did. We would all get in a line sitting on the floor facing the back of the person in front of us. Each person would massage the shoulders of the person in front for a few minutes, then someone would yell "TIME!" and the one in front would move to the back and we'd start all over again until everyone had had a massage. It was silly but lots of fun and you sure felt good afterward.

That night I thought to myself, "Boy! It would be sooooo nice to have a good backrub line going!" All of the sudden I realized that I NEEDED my husband!

I had come to a place where I was really comfortable with the fact that God was bringing my husband to me and that I didn't have to look all over for him. I was content, and I could have waited another couple of years. I knew that when the time was right, he would be brought to me.

I walked up the steps to the living room and the Spirit of God dropped on me like a blanket, and without so much as asking my permission, I found myself saying by the Spirit of God, "Husband, it is time for us to be together! Come forth in Jesus Name!" Immediately I thought, "How am I going to recognize him?" So I started to say to the Lord, "Lord, You tell me who...." Right there the Lord stopped me. It was as if He reached His arm down and laid a finger on my mouth and said, "Shhhh, don't say that." Immediately I realized what to say. It was, "Lord, you tell him who I am and have him come tell me." As soon as I said that, the anointing lifted and I went on about my business, promptly forgetting about it. It was one of the few things I forgot to write in my journal. That was at the end of July or the first week or two of August 1983.

I started work for Rhema that August, and at the same time was moving into a house with my best friend, Leslie, and planning a ministry trip to the East Coast with Keith, a dear friend.

Keith and I had gone to Rhema together. There was a time when we both wondered whether we were to be husband and wife and discussed it, but we never moved on anything. We just used to have so much fun together and would sit and talk about spiritual things for long hours. The challenge I had was that he was 16 years younger than me; but God had already dealt with me that spring that I was in fact going to marry someone younger than myself.

I was doing a self-image seminar for my former pastor, Patrick Bowen, who had moved to New Jersey, and Keith came with me to hold a Children's Crusade. We were sitting at a restaurant working on last minute details and another friend came in. We said hi and he asked to speak to me alone. He said to me, "I just walked through the door and the Lord spoke to me when I saw you. He said to tell you...beware of counterfeits. I immediately knew he was talking about my friend. So I stopped pondering the thought of his being my spouse.

We went to the East Coast and ministered. I came home and there was a note pinned to the front door from Paul.

Reflections from Samantha

The dream I had years before, the Words of Knowledge that had been given to me, God speaking to me and telling me that I was going to marry an "Okie," the street lights going off and coming on in the park, all the things that God spoke to my heart about my husband—God was moving me toward my destiny to marry the one man that would be my life companion.

For those of you believing God for that one person to spend the rest of your life with, it is important for you to know that God wants the best for you. He wants to bless you. He created you; He knows your personality, your likes, your dislikes, He knows what makes you special. Not only that but He knows who will be that one person who will bring out the very best in you and vice versa, and He wants to bring that person to you.

What God wants you to do is to trust Him and put your faith in Him. I love Mark 11:22, which says, "...have faith in God." Have faith in His ability to do what He said. Numbers 23:19 states: "God is not a man that he should lie; hath he said and shall he not do it? or hath he spoken and shall he not make it good?" God had spoken certain things to me and I knew that He would bring to pass those that He spoke to me.

Now it's your turn to put your faith in God's ability to bring to you those secret desires of the heart—that companion who will have the same heart and life goals that you have. God is not going to bring you someone way out in left field. He's not going to bring you someone you're not physically attracted to or someone who does not love the Lord as you do. It's your job to live close to the heart of God. It's your job to plug in to those things He's called you to do.

At the beginning of my first year at Rhema, a male friend was advising me on "finding a mate." He said, "Samantha! If you're going to "find" a man, you have to go where the men are! He suggested the Full Gospel Business Men's Association and told me where several groups met. I remember being distressed at the time thinking, "How in the world can I do that? I was in school four hours every day and I worked from 1 pm till 10 pm Monday through Friday. I didn't have a car at the time and relied on other people for transportation, so sometimes I didn't get home until midnight or later. That left Saturdays, which were reserved for studying, washing, etc. Sundays were spent traveling to Vian with the pastor and his wife for Sunday services. We often didn't get back until midnight and then it was start the week all over again. Where was I going to get time to "find" a man? I cried out to God! "God what do I do?" Instantly, two things came to my heart. God said, "He who finds a wife finds a good thing" (Prov. 18:22). Of course! I didn't have to go looking! God would have him find me! The second thing He said to me was, "Samantha, he will have a heart for the same things you have a heart for. All you have to do is be found doing what I've told you to do and be where I've told you to be. I will bring him across your path." There is a wonderful peace just being found doing what God has called you to do. You don't have to look here and look there, constantly asking, "God? Is this the one? Is that one it?" No. Rest, God created the universe; it is a small thing for Him to bring your spouse to you.

Now, a word to you men. Just because the Bible says he who finds a wife...does not mean you go looking for that wife. It does mean that you look to God to bring you across the path of your wife. You trust God to speak to your heart as to who your wife is. It does not mean that you date every girl in your work place, church—worse yet...church hop, or the internet to see "if this is the one." That's sort of like playing the lottery—it's a hit or miss thing. If you will trust God and also be found doing the things He has told you to do, He knows how to maneuver your path to cross hers. The most important thing for both of you is that you know God's voice. Do you recognize when He's speaking to your heart, or are you so busy doing for God that you don't spend time with Him, and hearing His voice is a hit or miss for you?

One of the things I have observed through the years in my own life and through others who want to be married is that we get in a hurry. The reason I ended up married to the wrong men was that I didn't pray. I didn't seek God. I wanted a man on my arm. Any man who paid attention to me I instantly thought I was in love with. I wasn't serving the Lord in those days. When I left Ray, and God told me I was going to be married again, it was vital that I marry the right man.

It is important that you marry the right one. Just because you've blown it in the past doesn't mean that you've missed God's best for your life. At any given time in your life, God has the right spouse for you. I know there are people that say we only have one right person to marry and if we miss it we'll have to settle for second best. Well, I can tell you that I haven't settled for second best. Everyday, I wake up and thank God for the wonderful man that God has given me. I can't even begin to imagine being married to someone else.

My first year at Rhema, during orientation, Pastor Ken and Lynette Hagin gave their testimony of how God had put them together. It was romantic and fun, and then she said something that caused me to have to think in a whole different direction. Paraphrasing what she said, "If you can imagine yourself being married to someone else, then you shouldn't marry that person. You have to think that he is the only person in the world for you."

My immediate reaction was, "How can you say that?" At that time I could think of all kinds of different types of men that I could be married to. Now, all these years later, I understand what she was saying. Yes, there are different men that you could marry and make it work, but at any given time in your life there is one person that is the very best for you. At the time of writing this book, I have been married to Paul for 25 years. I cannot imagine anyone more perfect, more wonderful, or more suited to me and me to him than Paul. Every day, he's more wonderful to me. Does that mean he's absolutely perfect? No! On occasion I've told him, "Paul, even when I am so angry with you I could spit nails, I still think you're the most wonderful man in the world." And you know what? I mean it with every fiber of my being.

At one point during my Rhema student days, there was a man I hung around with. We did things together with friends and as I watched him, he was fun, he loved God, and he treated me with respect. We talked a lot about Godly things. My heart was so hungry for a Godly relationship that I began to think that perhaps he was my husband. It came to a point where I really thought he was my husband. There was a problem however. He wanted something different in a wife than what I was. He wanted small and petite; I was tall and larger. He wanted a wife who was a stay at home mom; I was an on the go for ministry person. I found myself trying to change myself to fit what he wanted. Of course there was no way I could be that person. I kept trying anyway. I started putting pressure on in prayer. "Oh God! Show him, I'm his wife!" I would pray.

One day my roommate told me that my friend had almost asked me to marry him several times but still hadn't. That just stirred me to more prayer until one day as I started to pray for him to recognize that I was his wife, I began to have a vague uneasiness. The Lord spoke to me and told me I was trying to usurp someone's will and in essence practicing witchcraft. He instructed me not to put a name on that person but to pray that the person God had for me would hear clearly and obey. I will forever be grateful that my friend did not ask me to marry him. As terrific a friend as he was, he was not my spouse. He later married a wonderful girl, perfectly suited to him.

I did begin praying in line with how God told me to pray. As I was obedient to pray, God was able to move on my behalf. And work He did.

One Night In The Desert, GOD SAID...

One Night in the Desert

When God Speaks, It is Time to Listen
Paul, 1983

It was now July of 1983. I had not seen Samantha in seven months; I didn't know where she was or if she was even still in Tulsa. We had not talked in quite a while. As far as I was concerned there never was anything with her. I knew there was a big attraction, but we never entered into a serious relationship. We never touched, held hands, or even discussed marriage—one time at a Fourth of July party at my parents, we discussed what we were looking for in life and in marriage. We discussed where we were going and wanted with our lives but that was the extent of our relationship. In those seven months, I thought about Sam from time to time, but I was busy with the church group in Mustang and busy with my own kids. To be honest, I really didn't think she was my wife. In July of 1983, we were literally in two different worlds. She had traveled to the East Coast doing her thing, and I had gone to the West Coast to pick up my son and Keelie, his half sister, and immediately returned to Oklahoma where the kids and I had a month-long visit.

Around this time, there had been a lot of talk and discussion about my getting married. Two friends of mine, Rodney Brown and Craig Stanley, had ministered to me about my future wife and some other things. In addition, at a baptismal service where I baptized several in my dad's swimming pool including my son, James and Keelie, a lady named Betty McCormick, who was dripping wet from just being baptized, shared with me that she had had a dream about my wedding and described the wedding to me. I had a hard time grasping what she said. I kept asking her, "My what?" She would repeat the description of "my" wedding.

Later in August, the kids and I loaded up in my brother's "blue van" and left for California to take them home. Rodney went with us to help drive and keep me company. I had set up several preaching engagements in California and was planning to stay in the area for two or three weeks before returning to Oklahoma.

As I was driving, I was praying and trying to get myself ready for the meetings I had scheduled. I was just having a wonderful time with God. I was driving through the desert somewhere in Arizona around one or two in the morning. Rodney and the kids were asleep in the back of the van. I was getting into conversational prayer, thinking about what these people were saying about my getting married because there literally was nobody I was interested in, thinking about, or even dating. So I was driving, and in my mind I was thinking, "Well, why not ask God, He's told me other things."

I'd been praying in the Spirit for miles and miles, so I posed my thoughts as a question and asked God, "Lord, who's my wife?" And over my shoulder somebody spoke "Samantha." I looked back at Rodney and the kids, thinking maybe someone in the back seat was answering my question, but they were all still asleep. There was no doubt that I heard someone speak the name Samantha. I mean it was so audible and loud. I thought I heard it with my physical ears, but realized I had heard it through my spiritual ears.

Brother Hagin used to talk about how sometimes God would do that to him. The voice would be so loud He would turn around to see who was talking because it was so real. That's what happened to me. I was driving with both hands on the steering wheel, and my eyes were like saucers. I realized, "Oh my gosh, He just told me," and I was sitting there thinking, "Samantha." At that moment, I knew that I knew that I knew that it was Samantha. I took a deep sigh, and I said, "Yes, it is Sam."

I entered into a rest. That moment in my mind, I became married to Samantha. The wondering was over! I had felt God's presence in the past; I'd felt a move of God; I'd felt gifts; but I'd never felt this before in my life. As I sat there driving, the glory of God came into the van! I was almost afraid to move as the presence of God filled the van. I found myself saying with a holy reverence, "This is a holiness," and that's what it was.

I don't remember driving because of this glorious experience with God. I was weeping and praising all at the same time. The glory was on me for miles.

Later I thought, "My gosh as many mistakes as we make, God always gives us His best when we trust Him. No matter how big, how bad, or how wrong our mistakes in the past, God's plans for our lives are untainted. Satan had been working hard to convince me that because I had failed God, I would have to accept His "Plan B" for my life. Satan desperately wanted me to believe that God would use me but in some lesser, recycled manner. Satan's message was convincing. I had to settle for a wife less than what God had originally planned. I had somehow forfeited God's first choice for a wife. Somehow I thought I couldn't have the one that was going to be the good one, so I'd have to settle for someone else of lesser quality. Even in the ministry, I felt like the ministry was not going to be what God had originally planned because I'd blown it so badly and I'd failed God. But I guarantee you that Samantha was not a second rate wife! I promise you that!

Although I didn't break out singing the Halleluiah Chorus, I broke out singing, and sang in the Spirit for a long time. I was surprised I did not wake up Rodney and the kids. Somehow they slept through all of it. I got to California, and I didn't say anything to anybody about my experience.

Because of my Baptist up-bringing, I had these ideas about what a traditional preacher's wife would be. Samantha did not fit the traditional stereotype. I had to ask myself, "Can I release her to be the woman of God that He has called her to be?" "Am I intimidated by her?" "Can I share the pulpit with her?" I was at peace that I could answer all these questions with a resounding "Yes."

While I was in California, some of my friends, unknown to me, tried to set me up with another woman and had her over for dinner. I wasn't interested. I knew my future wife was somewhere in Oklahoma waiting for me. And so, I said goodbye to the kids and came back to Oklahoma. When I returned, I still did not mention my experience to anybody. I took covert action, and through my brother, Curtis, I tried to find out where Sam was. I would nonchalantly ask questions such as, "Do you know where Sam is? Have you seen Sam? Or, have you been in contact with her?" Always to my frustration, the answer was, "No."

Curtis and I had a mutual friend living in Broken Arrow who was in a relationship with a guy who was bad news. So, Curtis and I decided we needed to go up and talk to her—of course, I thought this would be a good excuse to go with the ulterior motive of finding out about Sam. Curtis and I made the trip to Broken Arrow and I tried to call Sam, but we still couldn't find her. Finally, we tracked her down. We drove by the address and looked in the window. You could see there was a bunch of furniture everywhere, and it was obvious someone was moving in. Well, I just left a note on the door.

Reflections from Paul

It was important to me to be lead of God and to know I had heard Him in my spirit. I did not trust myself to make a decision because of the many mistakes and wrong decisions I had made listening to my emotions and flesh telling me who my wife was. When Samantha came into my life, I told myself she wasn't my wife for all the wrong reasons.

I learned that night out in the desert that when you learn to trust and hear your spirit that God speaks to you through your spirit. You will find that when you know you've heard God, your emotions will line up with the will of God and your spirit.

I don't believe that everyone will have or even need what I call a "burning bush" experience. I did because of my past. Whatever you need, God is faithful to make His will known to you.

One of our biggest problems is that we're often not patient and we try to rush things and make things happen. That's when Satan can introduce those counterfeits into lives. Faith works on the outside, and patience works on the inside. It keeps your emotions in check. Patience keeps you from compromising your standards because patience is based on what it knows, based on the Word of God. It helps you to stand and remain in faith.

And God Said, "Let the Romance Continue"

A Romantic Journey Down a Bumpy Road

By now you are surely wondering what was in the note left on Samantha's door. That note is the end of wilderness wandering and the beginning of enjoying a land full of milk and honey. That note signifies that the journey to Rhema was over, but God's plan was just beginning to unfold. We would love to tell you that Paul found Samantha, lifted her up in his arms and carried her off into the sunset living happily ever after. The next chapter is far from a fairy tale. Just because God told Paul that Sam was his wife didn't mean that Sam took the message, dropped everything, got married, and set up housekeeping with Paul. God's confirmation kept Paul devoted to Sam, but the journey to the altar would be a bit bumpy.

After leaving the note and ministering to our friend, we came back to El Reno. During the week Sam called me, and we made plans to meet the following weekend. I had explained to Sam that I needed to come back to check on our friend.

That Saturday morning I called Sam and set up a time to come by and spend some time with her. I had to first give an estimate on a fencing job which had taken longer than I had expected. I called Sam again and told her I was running a little bit late and told her about when I would be in town.

(Samantha) I got off the phone and told my roommate that was Paul and that he'd be running a little bit late. When Paul told me he was coming up it occurred to me that he probably wanted me to get the gang together.

I thought to myself, "You know what, I am not calling anybody. That man is going to sit down and have a serious conversation with me. Up to then, Paul was always joking and light-hearted in his conversation. I really didn't know anything about him. Somehow it was important to me to know what his goals in life were. Where was he going with his life? What was important to him in life? Aside from that one walk under the lights and a short conversation at his mom and dad's that one summer, I knew very little about him. To me, at the time, friends knew about one another. They knew their likes, dislikes, their goals in life, heart desires and such. I thought to myself, this man is a friend, and friends talk to one another in more than jokes and laughter. So I determined not to call anybody until I had drawn a serious conversation out of him.

Leslie, my roommate, asked me why he was coming up, and my mind flashed back to an instance when Curtis, Paul, and I were driving in his mom and dad's car, and I was sitting in the middle. Paul had his arm up on the back of the seat, and it fell on my back, and he never moved his arm. I remember holding my breath wondering what was going on.

I had never dated Paul, and we certainly had never discussed marriage, but up out of my spirit, I said, "Leslie, I have the strangest feeling he's coming up to ask me to marry him." And then I got so embarrassed. I remember thinking, "Well you brazen hussy, where do you think you got that from." So I laughed and apologized to Leslie, and said, "Leslie, I don't know where that came from. I think he's coming up to minister to a couple that he knows."

(Paul) I was really excited about seeing Sam again—remember it had been about seven months. I never once thought, "Do I love her?" I never asked that question. I just had such a glorious experience with God that I knew it was God's will that we get married, and that was all that mattered.

I finally got on the road and headed up to see Sam, and then it really hit me on the turnpike. Here I was on my way, and I had no idea what I was going to say. I mean, how do you tell a woman God told you that she was your wife? I mean, this woman was special, and she was like, wow! I couldn't just say, "I

109

hope you don't have plans for next weekend because, well, we are getting married."

As I drove up the turnpike at 75 miles an hour, I was praying as fast as I could, sweating bullets and thinking, "We're getting married, how do I do it right off the bat here, and what do I do?" The Lord calmly said, "Find out where she is; find out where her head is; find out what's going on with her." With those comforting words, I at least knew how to begin the conversation. I had to admit, God's way made far more sense than, "Hi, how have you been, by the way, did I mention on the phone we're getting married?"

Sam had just recently gone to work for Rhema and my life was pretty well planned out, so in my mind I was thinking, "Well if we get married, she'd be moving down to El Reno." I was trying to get it all worked out in my head.

I finally get there. I walked to the door of her house, and when I saw her I said, "Whoa!" She had lost a lot of weight, and she was looking mighty good.

Whenever I was with Sam in the past, I never would talk seriously with her; it was always surface chit-chat and kidding around because until I knew who my wife was, I was never going to let another woman inside my head. Several times Sam tried to talk to me and I would quickly get away from her because I wasn't going to let another woman down in my heart and open myself up until I met the right woman. And now, here I was, asking questions, and trying to get serious. I knew Samantha was wondering what had gotten into me.

(Sam) My thought was, "Boy, who plugged you in?"

(Paul) It was time to find out where she was and what she wanted out of life. We talked and finally I asked, "Well what would you like to do?"

(Samantha) I told Paul, "I haven't called anybody."

(Paul) I responded, "That's alright. I really just wanted to see you."

(Sam) I was surprised. I said, "Oh! You mean this is a date?"

(Paul) She was all surprised that we had a date. So we went to a movie and enjoyed it—a James Bond movie, Never Say Never. From the movie we went out to Denny's Restaurant. As we pulled into Denny's, one of the big light poles with all the lights on it went off. I leaned forward looking over the steering wheel and wondered what in the world was going on because that one light pole with multiple lights darkened the whole section of that parking lot. We went indoors, and from where we were standing inside waiting to be seated, I looked out and the light came back on. I looked at people walking by the light and nothing happened—we knocked out yet another set of lights.

We sat visiting, talking, and having a good time when two of her friends came walking by the table. Sam introduced me to them. They told us later that they walked away from the table agreeing that if Sam didn't marry me, she was crazy. It appears that virtually everybody that had seen us together that night came to us after we were engaged and told us pretty much the same thing.

God had signs along the way saying "This is Me pay attention," and I was blithely going along too busy to pay attention. Everybody but us knew we were supposed to be together—even my mother. I remember when I came home and told her we were engaged; she said that she told one of the kids that when Sam first came down to visit if I ever got married it would be to Sam.

I was running out of subjects to talk about, and I was getting down to where I had to bring up the subject of marriage. Finally I thought of one more thing to talk about. "Tell me about New Jersey. How were the meetings out there?" She burst out laughing.

(Sam) Like I explained earlier, I had gone to New Jersey to minister. While I was out there Patrick ordained me. There was a sweet, young man who was 24 years old—I had just turned 39—who came up to me after the service and said, "Now don't say anything, but God has told me that you're my wife."

(Paul) Sam was telling me this story, and she couldn't stop laughing about her strange proposal. I sat there speechless as all my courage went right out the window. As I sat there my mind was telling me, "Oh my gosh, she's just going to laugh at me when I tell her, 'You know, that's what I'm here for. I am here to tell you that you're my wife.'" I was devastated and lost my courage to talk about her becoming my wife.

We left the restaurant and drove back out to the Western Village that we had been to the summer before. We went over to some benches really close to the Village and talked a little bit. Finally, I realized I was sighing and had done it about four times. Sam was really silent. She didn't say anything, and I realized she knew something was going on. I sighed once more and finally said, "Samantha, I've got to tell you something. I had an experience with God, and I need to tell you what happened. I backed up a little bit to what Rodney and Craig Stanley had said, then what Betty had said, then the dream I had had, and finally I told her what God had told me in the desert. I told her what I had prayed and how God had told me it was her—she was my wife.

She was dead silent—thankfully, she didn't burst out laughing, but oh, was I nervous. But, the Lord had told me on the drive up, don't just go up there and try to corner her. Leave her a way out. I

113

said, "If I have heard God, then we need to be praying about it." She kind of agreed.

(Sam) Surprisingly, my heart was not going pitter patter. I was just very calm. I was thinking it probably was God, but I wasn't remembering all the stuff over the years that God had told me. I had totally forgotten the night that the Lord told me how I would recognize him. I remembered what I'd said a little bit earlier that day. Of course, I already thought he was the most handsome thing I had ever seen; he was hunk city, and my heart raced when I thought about him.

I remembered what the Lord had said to me earlier in the day when I had driven Leslie to work. On the way back to get ready for Paul, I kept smiling and I kept trying to wipe the smile off my face. I told myself, "Samantha, just relax; he's just coming to talk to this couple—but that silly smile would come back, and I'm thinking to myself, "I get to see Paul! I'm going to see the hunk!" The Lord spoke up and said, "Just relax. It's Okay to be excited about his visit." That was enough for me to say to him, "Well, let's head that direction. I still need to pray though. You've heard God, but I need to hear God too. Let's not tell anyone until I'm sure."

It never even occurred to me to ask myself, "Do I love this man?" The question that I pondered was, "What is God saying? Is this God? Is God saying this to us?" Because, if this was the will of God, I knew I liked him and thought he was wonderful, and yes, I could see myself as Paul's wife.

I just had to back up from everything. I am usually one of those people who plunges into everything and goes where angels fear to tread. But this was marriage, for me a third marriage. It was really important not to make a mistake again. I had to make sure.

(Paul) We left the park and headed back toward her place. Sam finally responded. She consented to head that direction on the condition that we didn't tell anybody. That commitment lasted until I got back to El Reno—as soon as I got home, I started telling everybody.

She had told me about the ledger she had been keeping, and showed it to me. Over the last several years, God had been giving her things about her husband. God would describe his personality and character—a little about his looks but mostly the kind of man he was. She would write them down and date them, so there were several pages. When we got to her house, she handed the ledger to me and I started reading it.

It was the weirdest thing because, as I'm reading, I'm reading a description of me. Page after page, different dates, and different times, but the description is ME.

(Sam) Leslie had met us at the door, and we told her what was going on. She knew about my journal and wanted Paul to see it. I hesitated. I didn't want him to see it since I wasn't sure if this was God, but I went ahead and showed it to him. When Paul finished reading it Leslie said, "Ok Samantha, write down...His name is Paul Roach." I wrote it down, but only because they were both watching me, and I didn't know what else to do.

(Paul) Before I left we had our first kiss, we literally talked marriage, got engaged (sort of)—it was about 4:00 a.m.—and I kissed her. This is weird too because I never once thought or asked myself do I love this woman? I kissed her, and down in my spirit something happened. It felt like something dropped into me. I stepped back, looked down at myself and it was love! In an instant I fell in love with her. It started down in my spirit and flooded through me. I looked up at her and said "I'm in love with you." She gave me the weirdest look like WHAT?

(Sam) I didn't know what to do or say. I knew I really liked him, but because I hadn't remembered all that God had said to me, I was afraid to commit to it without having a "come to Jesus meeting with God" and having God speak to me absolutely and clearly that this was His will for me. I finally looked at him and said, "Oh, well ok" because I could not say I love you.

(Paul) I fell in love with her just like that, God did it, it was a God thing, I kissed her and I stepped back and it was like...BAM; it just fizzed through me and I said I love you; I fell in love with her in just a matter of seconds, and I had not even thought about it or asked myself whether I loved her; I just fell in love with her, and I knew it was God. It was like WOW!

I left about 4:30 a.m., and then picked her up about 9:30 a.m. that morning and went to her church, Walnut Grove Church.   David Ingles, the Gospel singer, was the pastor. When we walked in, every eye in the place was on me. I've never had so many holes stared or bored through me in my life. It was like every time I turned around and looked in the room nobody was looking at the preacher or paying attention to him; nobody was hearing him; everybody was staring at us with the same question tattooed on their foreheads: who is this man with Sam?

David Ingles wife, Sharon, and Sam were good buddies, and we walked up and Samantha introduced me as her fiancée. I was expecting something like, "Glory hallelujah, isn't this wonderful!"   Instead, Sharon turned and looked at me with an intense look and said, "Where are you taking her?" I knew I was in trouble, I gulped, "Oh my gosh," and backed up a little and said "Well, I...I...I.."

(Sam) I was doing singles activities at Walnut Grove at that time. We had really worked hard to get

117

the singles department functioning, and I'm sure she didn't want anything to mess that up.

(Paul) I drove back to El Reno that Sunday evening and promptly told everyone that Sam and I were engaged.

(Sam) I went back to work at Rhema that Monday under a really busy schedule. That Tuesday night I got a phone call from Curtis. When I answered the phone, Curtis instantly said, "Congratulations!" I immediately was in turmoil and said, "Oh! Curtis! He wasn't supposed to say anything!"

(Paul) Curtis turned ashen gray, wiped the smile off his face, and silently handed the phone back to me. Sam sounded really distressed and reminded me I wasn't supposed to tell anybody. I don't think she took into account that we had already told Pastor David and Sharon plus her roommate Leslie. In any event, she said she was going to fly down that Saturday night to talk to me.

(Samantha) I made a reservation to fly down to talk, but really, my intent was to call off the "semi-engagement."

(Paul) I went into several days of fasting and prayer. They were the most miserable days of my life. I cried out to God, "O God! Show this woman, get a hold of her; show her what you've shown me!" As I walked around the family farm praying, trying not to panic, the Lord spoke to me and said, "Become her best friend."

(Sam) That whole week was so busy. I hardly had time to turn around and breath. That year, instead of a "Fall Social" that Rhema usually had, we put together a school picnic with lots of fun things for everyone to do. Then I left immediately from the picnic to fly to Oklahoma City to meet Paul.

(Paul) I picked her up, and it was strained and reserved talking as we drove to El Reno. I took her to the most romantic place El Reno has—a lake that overlooks the Federal Prison. I was hoping the lights from the prison reflecting on the water would soften her heart. We sat and talked. I let her know all that was in my heart, and let her get to know the real me.

That Sunday afternoon, I had to check on some fences I was building, and I took Samantha with me. She began to ask me questions. I would answer them the best I knew how, but then she would ask the same question in a different way—not one but several different ways. I kept trying to answer the questions in different ways, but I was running out of ways to answer her. By then, I was frustrated and thinking, "God! Are you sure? If this is the way it's going to be, I don't think I can handle this!"

(Sam) I was trying to think of ways to call things off, but every time I started to, I would delay it with some inane question, trying to get a handle on what his goals in life were, how he envisioned his life, and did he have a plan for success in his life. Finally out of frustration, he said to me, "Samantha, I know who I am, but I really don't think you know who I am." That was true. In the times we had seen one another, it was always in a group, and we just joked and teased around. I never knew what was in him. I didn't know the goals he had in life or how he planned to achieve those goals. I was so desperate not to marry a failure. I didn't equate that God was bringing my husband and He would not bring me a failure.

I finally settled down some and as we're still riding along in the truck, up out of my spirit came a David Ingles song, "I Sure Love You." I had gone down there to call the engagement off, not tell him I love him! Again, about three times the first words of that song rose in my heart. Finally I realize it was God, and I sang the first line of the song. "I sure love You, I sure love You...." to my surprise, Paul chimes in and helps me sing the rest of the verse, "You are marvelous, You're wonderful and I love You. Thank You for all You have done...especially for the gift of Your Son...I sure love You." Brother David wrote it as a love song to the Lord, but the Lord had us sing it to one another, and we sang the last line as "....especially for the gift of THIS ONE...I sure love you." Well, I couldn't call it off that weekend!

The next weekend I had to take Rhema students to Eureka Springs, Arkansas to the Passion Play. So now, I break the "code of silence" and tell several of the girls on the trip. Word spread through the bus like wildfire, and as we returned to the shopping mall parking lot where everyone was to meet his ride, Paul was also there to pick me up. Immediately, everyone on the right side of the bus went to the left side of the bus where they all peered out the window looking at Paul. I watched this and all I could think of was, "Oh God! Is the bus going to tip over?"

(Paul) During the weeks to come I would pray, and God would tell me what to do the next weekend while I was with her. Each week she would be in turmoil, but the Lord would tell me what to say and how to minister to her, and it would bring her peace.

As I waited for the bus to arrive the Lord spoke to me and I knew that we had to go back to the little Western Village and pray. I didn't know what about; I just knew that as soon as she got off that bus, we had to go pray.

The bus arrived and I was excited to see her, I looked up at the bus and suddenly every window was full of people peering out the windows staring at me and checking me out. I wondered if I passed muster! She got everybody off the bus and off to their respective destinations, and I finally had her to myself. We drove off to the Western Village.

It was a nice fall, late afternoon, and the park had several people in it, so I took her to an area of trees and leaned against one and took her in my arms and started to pray. As I did so, the same holiness that fell on me in the desert fell on me that afternoon. It was the first time in my life it was a holy act to take a woman in my arms. As I stood there sensing this purity and holiness settle on us like a blanket, I heard myself speaking words of commitment to her. I told her, "This day I choose to be a husband to you. I choose to honor you as a wife. I choose to protect you. I choose to wash you with the water of the Word. I choose to love you and to give my life for you as Christ gave his life for the church."

(Samantha) As Paul drew me to himself, I too felt that holiness. It was just like a spiritual blanket had dropped on us. It was as though we were all alone in the universe in the presence of God. I remember thinking; "This must be what it was like in the Garden of Eden before Adam and Eve ever sinned—a purely sinless state." Then Paul began speaking to me. It was a strong, powerful anointing on him as he spoke. Each time he would say, "I choose..." it seemed as though a heavy brick would fall off my shoulders, first one, then another, until there was lightness and a joy bubbling up in me. I heard the Lord say to me, "This day you became his wife." I thought at the time that it was an odd way to put it. It was later that it became

122

clear what He meant. That weekend brought me enough peace to continue.

What Paul had not known was that the summer between my first and second year at Rhema, the school I worked for sent me to Dallas, Texas to fill in as director of a vocational school that had had some problems. I had been asking the Lord questions about the role of a husband to his wife and the role of a wife to her husband.

Friends had been telling me that I was just too strong a woman and that men did not want strong women or at least not women who showed that strength. They said I wasn't a very submissive person. That really bothered me because having lived with Ray, I had learned to be very submissive, in the sense of obeying his every word for fear of dying if I didn't. So I had asked the Lord, "Is that true? Am I not a very submissive person? Do I need to pretend to be something I'm not? That summer I attended a church in Dallas that Pastor Joe Nay started. One Sunday they had a wedding after the service and invited everyone to stay and witness it. I didn't have anything to do, so I stayed. Pastor Nay began describing the husband/wife relationship and the passage of scripture, Ephesians 5. Now two and one-half years later, Paul was speaking those words to me. It filled my heart with peace—at least for a little while.

The next weekend Paul stayed with his friend, Kirk, and told him that we were engaged. I had given notice to Rhema that I would be leaving. I didn't want to leave, but I had been taught that you always went wherever your husband was. It never occurred to me that I was to pray and hear God, or that God might have a different plan. I had never dated, let alone, married a Christian man. I didn't know how any of that worked.

(Paul) Kirk and his wife Pat were excited, and they made arrangements to meet us for lunch after the Sunday service. As we arrived at the restaurant and were seated, I noticed that many of the waiters and waitresses were staring at us and talking. One of them came over to us and said, "Boy, you must be somebody important!" I looked at him and said, "Oh? Why's that?" He pointed to several of the servers and said, "They're all Rhema students, and they recognize you."

(Samantha) My job at Rhema was a fun, high profile job. I got paid to make sure they all played. At that time in Rhema's history, students came to school very serious. They were intent on getting an education and going out to win the world, which was all right and good. In the process, however, they were so intense that somehow laughing and relaxing was not part of the picture. It often caused them to become rigid and out of balance. So I was often on stage doing something funny or silly and was easily recognizable. It was difficult to go anywhere without being recognized, but that was true of the teachers and everybody that worked at Rhema.

(Paul) Our orders were finally taken, and Kirk spoke to me and said, "I prayed about you guys last night, and I think it's God's will for you to be married." I thought to myself, "Well thanks, Kirk." He continued, "The Lord said to tell you something. You're to consider coming up here." I immediately started to lift my hand to say, "No! No!" As I raised my hand and opened my mouth to say no, I literally could not say anything. I put my hand down and realized that the Lord had shut my mouth. I thought, "Oh my gosh." I knew that something had just happened, but I wasn't sure what.

A thousand thoughts were going through my head. "I may be moving up here! What am I going to do? My life is set in El Reno; I'm pastoring there; what about the people?" Questions and no answers, I was in turmoil. After we left Kirk and Pat, I turned to Samantha and asked her what she thought.

(Samantha) I wouldn't tell him what I thought. I felt like he had to hear God for himself. The summer after Curtis and I graduated, he and I had a conversation about Paul. We had sensed that he was supposed to go to Rhema, but it wasn't something either of us felt comfortable telling him, so we prayed that God would speak to him about attending Rhema if the Lord was intent on his going.

Now Paul was asking me what I thought. I didn't know what to do because I was definitely not used to having that kind of influence in a man's life. I knew that one of the reasons I had been hesitant about marrying him was because Rhema had had such a major life changing impact on my life (as it does all who attend), and I agreed wholeheartedly with what Dad Hagin and Pastor Hagin taught. I couldn't see myself married to someone who did not fall into the Rhema camp. I wasn't sure that Paul agreed with them. I knew I wanted him to go and felt like he should go, but he had to know it for himself. So I told him he had to pray and hear God for himself.

(Paul) I left to head back to El Reno. Driving the I-44 Turnpike took a couple of hours each way, and I had gotten into the habit of praying. So I prayed and asked the Lord about Kirk's statement. I knew that if God was having me move to Tulsa that it wasn't just for Samantha. I knew that she loved Rhema, but God would have a reason for me to be there too. As I drove and prayed, he laid out the plans he had for my life. He said, "I'm putting you back in school. You're going to go to Rhema. You will help David Ingles and become his youth pastor and do whatever he needs you to do."

(Samantha) I was thrilled that he was going to come up there. First, because I knew we'd be on the same page as far as our beliefs, and second, because I would still get to work at Rhema.

(Paul) We were going along pretty well, still having a few times of fear on Samantha's part, but I would drive up, and she would be at peace and the fear would leave. We had actually scheduled a wedding date, May 19th. That January of 1984, we had scheduled a Self-Image Seminar for Samantha to do in El Reno. She and her roommate Leslie came down and did the seminar. Leslie drove back to Tulsa, and I drove Samantha back a day later.

As we were driving back, she was sitting with her back against the passenger window and her legs stretched out and on my lap. She was beginning to ask questions again.

(Samantha) As I sat there, I asked, "Tell me again how you see a marriage." He began to describe to me what he felt a marriage should be. I was listening but my mind began to wander. All of the sudden the Spirit of God spoke to me sharply and said, "Samantha! Pay attention! There are thousands of women who would love to hear what this man is saying, but he is saying it to you!" He had my attention at that point.

(Paul) Suddenly, I sensed that a wall had come down in her, and I began to pray in the Spirit. I sensed an anointing come on me, and I began to bind a lying spirit and command it to come off her.

(Samantha)   As he started praying, I felt a heavy weight come off my chest, and a black cloudy form went...swoosh...out the window. What he didn't know was that because I had been burning the candle at both ends, I hadn't spent the time in prayer that I needed to. I was emotionally and spiritually struggling. Sometimes in the middle of the night, I would wake up and find that I wasn't breathing. I would have to mentally say to myself, "Samantha! Breathe!" I would take a breath and then I would be okay. When we got to my house, I was thinking about what the Lord had said to me, on the turnpike, and what Paul had said, and with that spirit off me, I told the Lord quietly, "Lord, I will marry Paul on May 19th no matter what!"

The Lord spoke to me and said, "This day Paul became your husband." Immediately I understood what had happened that day at the Western Village when the Lord said to me, "This day you became his wife." Paul had chosen that day to become my husband. He had chosen to take on the responsibility of a Godly husband. Now, three months later I had chosen to take Paul as my husband. I had chosen to be a wife to him and all that entailed. I knew on that day, January 31st, 1984, that he was my husband. So I turned to him and told him that I would marry him on

May 19th, 1984 no matter what! There were a few struggles from time to time that he had to help me pray through and it was getting easier and easier to stay at peace.

There was one point where a friend came over and began telling me all the struggles she had had about marrying someone and the struggle of image and whether they would be a successful couple. I immediately began to think about whether Paul and I had the same goals in life and began to have a major anxiety attack. I remember going over to Pastor David and Sharon's house and pouring out my heart to them. Sharon sat me down and asked David to sing one of his new songs to me. He sat at the piano and began to play, "I'm making plans to succeed! I'm making plans to succeed..." As he continued to sing, my heart settled down, and I got in agreement with what the Word said and Brother David's song..."I'm not making plans to fail. God did not bring us this far to fail...I'm making plans to succeed." That brought peace to my heart once again.

I finally knew that I knew that I knew that Paul was indeed the man whom God had chosen for me. I thank God every day for His patience and His grace and mercy toward me. He knew exactly what it would take for me to get it right.

Reflections from Paul

BOY!! Was I so glad that she finally heard from God and obeyed Him.

I want to address those of you who feel you made a wrong choice and married the wrong person. First of all, you're married. God recognizes it as a marriage and wants to bless it, so dedicate your marriage to him. Then, surround your mate with faith and love.

If for some reason your marriage does come apart, just remember, it is not the end of the world, and divorce is not the unpardonable sin. God will still bless you if you trust him. God is a God of new beginnings.

Dearly Beloved...

Will She Finally Make it Down the Aisle?

As I walked down the aisle, a thousand thoughts were going through my head. Mainly, my head was screaming, "I'm changing my life forever! Am I sure! Am I doing the right thing?" I had preached to others that when I married my "prince charming" I would walk down that aisle with joy in my heart, a skip to my step, to be joined forever to my one true love.

Instead, I was just like Paul said, scared and praying, "Oh God! Oh God! This is You isn't it?" There were about 400 people at the wedding—mostly Rhema students and Paul's family. On the one hand, I didn't know where to put my eyes, so many people, all so happy for us. I wanted to greet them all and thank them for sharing this wonderful day. On the other hand, I wanted to run away and hide, preferably to Africa and never come back.

Finally, my eyes focused on Paul, standing tall and handsome, and a peace settled on me—all the promises and precious words from the Lord came swirling around me and I knew...I KNEW! This man,

131

this kind, loving, joyful, Godly hunk of a man was God's special gift to His daughter who had cried out..."Lord! You choose him and bring him to me!"

I walked down the aisle, and Paul stepped down to take my hand. Patrick, my former pastor, who had flown in from New Jersey, spoke up and said, "Who gives this woman in marriage?" My father spoke up and said, "Her mother and I." Those simple words were the finishing touch on finally getting things right in my life. This day, on the day of my commitment for the rest of my life, all was right. I was surrounded by my parents and people I loved who watched the fulfillment of a miraculous joining of two lives, once broken, now healed and healthy, ready to face the next steps of our lives together.

Our Tribute

How Could We Say Thanks...

Reflecting back on the wedding is always a wonder of God's grace and provision. Here I was walking down the aisle meeting my prince, my knight in shining armor, which he was and is in my life, and I was still nervous. My thought was, "I'm changing my life forever! Do I want to do this?" When I finally stopped looking at all the people and turned my eyes on Paul, the man whom God had painted a picture of in my heart, was in front of me and he only had eyes for me. The wedding was everything a girl could want, surrounded by family and friends and people we loved.

When Paul and I got engaged officially, my immediate thought was, "How in the world can we have a large wedding?" Great question for a girl who had just been taught faith for two years solid at the greatest Bible school on planet earth! Where had I put my faith? Maybe we couldn't afford an expensive wedding, but my heavenly Father certainly could. I thought about my precious parents who would have given me whatever I needed had they had it. Suddenly, the Spirit of God spoke to me and said, "I'm your Father. I'll foot the bill for you!" I immediately started laughing and crying all in the same breath. Foot the bill He did!

I needed a wedding dress and accessories, and God provided. We needed a church for the wedding and God abundantly provided.

We wanted Patrick to come perform our wedding. Years before, while still attending Patrick's church in Vian, I saw him perform a wedding. It was so beautiful and so individualized that I said to him afterward, "Patrick, I don't care where I am, I want you to perform my wedding." God provided. Patrick later told me that the Lord spoke to him right then and said, "She is going to be getting married, and you are to perform her wedding ceremony."

We needed 800 wedding invitations—God provided. Next, we needed a place for the wedding reception and money to cover the cost of the reception—this was no problem for my Father.

We must remember that God is our Father, and He delights in providing for us. I love Psalms 35:27 "Let them shout for joy and be glad, that favor my righteous cause; yea, let them say continually, 'Let the Lord be magnified, which hath pleasure in the prosperity of his servants.'" God is more ready to bless us than we realize. I watched as God, my Father, provided one thing after another for us. When it was all said and done, God had footed the bill for the most wonderful wedding and reception that a girl could want. As we've written this book, I am so aware of His love and His provision for us. When fear would try to come, I would hear Him telling me, "I'm your Father, I'll foot the bill." I knew that I had to keep my eyes on the promise and not on the lack of money. Hebrews 11:6 says, "But without faith, it is impossible to please him..." When God gives you a promise, you're responsible to "keep the switch of faith turned on." He will provide when you keep your eye on Him.

We finally exchanged vows. We all had an opportunity to praise God and give Him the glory for all He had done to make this memorable day a reality. We had asked our good friend, Frank Yeager, a former Philadelphia Opera singer, to honor God on our behalf by singing Andrea Crouch's moving song, *My Tribute.* His angelic voice led us to the throne of God as we all lifted our hands in worship.

The words of that great hymn seem appropriate to revisit as we bring this story to a conclusion:

How can I say thanks for all the things You have done for me. Things so undeserved, but You died to prove Your love for me.

The voices of a million angels could not express my gratitude. All that I am, or ever hope to be, I owe it all to Thee.

To God be the glory, to God be the glory, to God be the glory for the things He has done!

After Frank sang that song the congregation broke out in shouts of praise and worship for several minutes. We said our vows and Patrick's wife gave a message in tongues and Patrick interpreted a prophecy. In the 25 years since, we've seen God's promises and the prophecy come to pass. How faithful God is.

Through It All

Celebrating 25 Years of Blessings

Robert Frost wrote, "I shall be telling this with a sigh somewhere ages and ages hence: Two roads diverged in a yellow wood and sorry I could not travel both, I took the one less traveled by and that has made all the difference."

As we look back over 25 of marriage, we are awed at the way God has led us through all the trials, tribulations, mountains, and valleys. Another song by Andrea Crouch, "Through It All," sums up our testimony to God and about God, here are the words, personalized:

We've had many tears and sorrows
We've had questions for tomorrow
There've been times we didn't know right from wrong
But in every situation God gave blessed consolation
That our trials only come to make us strong.
So we thank God for the mountains
And we thank Him for the valleys

We thank Him for the storms He's brought us through
'cause if we never had a problem
We wouldn't know that He could solve them
We wouldn't know what faith in His Word could do.
Through it all, through it all,
We've learned to trust in Jesus,
We've learned to trust in God.
Through it all, through it all,
We've learned we can depend upon His Word.

Final Reflections from Samantha

So the beautiful marriage ceremony and wedding reception was over. Now the marriage began. So what has happened in these 25 years of marriage?

Many people think that when God ordains a marriage and puts it together like He did ours, there will be no problems, no trials, and no tribulations. Every storybook romance ends with, "And They Lived Happily Ever After!" Even though that's the title of our next book I can tell you that just isn't so.

Paul and I can tell you there are trials and tribulations. There are ups and downs and challenges. Some of those times were our own fault, others because of situations thrust upon us that were difficult for us to walk through. Like the song at the beginning of this chapter, we have learned to trust God to forgive us, lead us, strengthen us and take us forward to victory.

The Lord spoke to Paul to go back to school—Rhema of course! So the September following our wedding Paul enrolled as a student. I was still on staff and loved my job. I was thrilled that we were staying. Paul was graduating and we had opportunity for Paul to go on staff also. Oh how we would have loved to stay, but it's very difficult to argue with God when your husband has an open vision and tells him to leave and start a church in San Diego. So off to California we went. Little did we know that God was working things out for Paul and his son.

Paul and I had prayed that God would work in such a way that he would be allowed to raise his son. About nine months after arriving in San Diego, James and his half sister, Keelie arrived in our home. We were ecstatic. I became an instant mom. I would love to say that I was a wonderful mother but there were challenges to raising a teenager and an eleven year old whose thoughts and ideas of life were already set differently than what I thought they should be. It was a very hard time for them and me. James has graciously long since forgiven me, and we have a wonderful relationship now, but at that time it was something I personally had to learn to trust God about.

Three years in San Diego as a pastor's wife was also challenging. Not only was I a new wife to a

Christian, which was totally different than being married to a non-Christian, but I had to learn what being a pastor's wife was all about also. Those 3 years I can truthfully say stretched me beyond anything I thought was possible...but again...through it all I learned that God was faithful to lead me, teach me, and love me in spite of myself.

The day came when the Lord sent us to Paul's hometown of El Reno, Oklahoma, where we have been for nearly 20 years. I have my 'sea legs' now so to speak, being a pastor's wife that is. I love being a pastor's wife and I love being married to Paul. I remembered Pastor Ken and Lynnette's statement all those years ago in my first year at Rhema about not being able to imagine yourself being married to anyone else. I understand that now. I know now what they meant. I watch my husband today as he ministers to people and he plays with our grandchildren and how he ministers to me and I am more in love with him today than ever before.

A marriage should be constantly growing and discovering everything good and wonderful about your mate. Of course you're going to have challenges, but I love something that Bruce Cook said in a video series called, "TEAMMATES". Learn to become your mate's greatest cheerleader. That became a byword for Paul and me.

In writing this book and remembering all the wonderful things that God did to bring Paul and I together and the subsequent years, I am chagrined at the many times that I panicked. There is a major lesson that all of us have to learn at one time or another. Some learn it, some don't. That lesson is what I call "The Busier than God Syndrome."

Concerning our engagement, there were neon signs everywhere, God shouting, "This is me! Pay attention!" The most important lesson you can learn from my mistakes is that it is more important to spend time with God than working for God. Yes, God loves what you do for Him and has even called you to that work, but the work for God needs to come out of the time spent with God. That place of fellowship is a place of peace, of hearing His voice, getting direction, strengthening and vision. If I had disciplined myself to spend that time of intimacy with the Lord I would not have struggled as I did. I would have remembered all the wonderful things God had told me. He would have unfolded it before me one miraculous word at a time until I saw the whole pictures. I would have been able to move confidently toward my future without all the panic and would have had a sense of joy at what God was doing.

Being busier than God robs you of peace, robs you of the knowing that comes from having spent time with the Lord, robs you of being able to hear God clearly, and robs you of confidence. Learn this one valuable lesson...spend time with the Lord daily. He's speaking to us all the time. We just have to learn to slow down and listen.

I love Philippians 2:13 which says, "For it is God which worketh in you both to will and to do of His good pleasure." The Lord took two broken lives that had failed Him miserably, forgave us, picked us up and worked in us both the want to and the ability to do of His good pleasure. He made us into something of value and worth. God is a restorer of the breaches. He never leads us to defeat. Second Corinthians 2:14 is another favorite scripture for me; and it says, paraphrased, "Now thanks be unto God who always causes us to triumph."

Paul and I are living examples of his love and mercy and people whom God has caused to triumph. If your life is in shambles, know of a surety that God can take your life, no matter how far down you feel, no matter how badly you've missed it and turn it for good.

Final Reflections from Paul

The Lord had spoken to me and told me I was to attend Rhema, which I did that Fall after Samantha and I married. I became an assistant pastor for David Ingles and worked with the youth. At the same time, Pastor David started a radio station, Oasis Network, which today reaches around the world that I had the privilege of helping with.

We had really wanted to stay in Tulsa and work with Rhema, but as Samantha said, I had an open vision and the Lord said go to San Diego and start a church. Little did we realize what God had in mind. We were there nearly a year when we received a phone call from Keelie, who wanted to come live with us. James came a few days later.

Keelie left after a year to return home to her mother and James stayed with us. We learned that he had prayed two things. The first was to be able to live with his dad and the second was to be able to live on the same farm that his dad was raised on.

When it came time for us to move to El Reno, my hometown, James moved with us. Again, God was working out plans that only He could work out. James was able to be around his grandparents, grow up on the farm, and be with his cousins who were all born within five months of each other. They went to school

143

together, played sports together and in general did all the things that close brothers and cousins do.

We've pastored here nearly 20 years. During that time we've seen our son graduate from high school, spend five and one-half years in the Navy, answer the call of God on his life, graduate from Rhema, marry a terrific girl, also a minister, and give us five wonderful grandchildren. They are associate pastors and minister to the youth in Weatherford, Oklahoma.

In all our years as pastors we have seen all the usual things that pastors see in a church and we are still blessed. We have a wonderful congregation, whom we love dearly. Our ties with Rhema remain strong. We are now serving as one of the Oklahoma District Directors for Rhema.

25 years of marriage! God has truly blessed us. There is very seldom a day that we don't thank God for the gift that He gave us in each other. To feel that love well up and fill us with such great joy often leaves us speechless and thankful beyond words for what God has done for us. We truly are more in love today than we were in the beginning.

How grateful I am that "One night in the Desert, God said...Samantha."

And God Said...

"I Now Pronounce You Husband and Wife"

Paul and Samantha Roach, May 19, 1984

It's Time...To Come Home To Jesus

If you've read this book and you are not born again—
That is, you have never prayed and asked the Lord Jesus
Christ into your heart—it's time. If you're born again, but
like us you have gotten off track...it's time to come home.

Jesus is waiting for you. He loves you and wants to
give you a wonderful life, full of his grace, mercy, and love.

It's simple really; from your heart just ask Him to
forgive you and cleanse you from all sin. The following
prayer is from Rodney Howard Browne's ministry, Revival
Ministries International. You can pray this prayer and
know that you've been forgiven and that Jesus has come
into your heart. Just pray this out loud:

*"Dear Lord Jesus, come into my heart. Forgive me of
my sin. Wash me and cleanse me. Set me free Jesus, thank
You that You died for me. I believe that You are risen from
the dead and that you are coming back again for me. Fill
me with the Holy Spirit. Give me a passion for the lost, a
hunger for the things of God and a holy boldness to preach
the gospel of Jesus Christ. I'm saved; I'm forgiven and I'm
on my way to Heaven because I have Jesus in my heart.*

Now that you've prayed from your heart and asked
Jesus into your heart, you need to tell somebody. Let
someone know that there's been a change in your life.
Choose now, to live for Christ. He gave His life for you, live
your life in such a way that people see Christ in you.

Find a good church! That's vital to your life being
victorious. It's true you don't have to go to church to be
saved, but the Bible says, "Forsake not the assembling of
yourselves together."

Printed in the United States
215796BV00002B/3/P